Warnow

Elbe

West Berlin   East Berlin
Berlin Wall

Spree

HARZ MOUNTAINS

THURINGIAN FOREST

ERZGEBIRGE

BAVARIAN FOREST

Isar

BAVARIAN ALPS

GERMANY

GERMANY

By the Editors of Time-Life Books

TIME-LIFE BOOKS ∘ ALEXANDRIA, VIRGINIA

TIME LIFE BOOKS

Other Publications:

FIX IT YOURSELF
FITNESS, HEALTH & NUTRITION
SUCCESSFUL PARENTING
HEALTHY HOME COOKING
UNDERSTANDING COMPUTERS
THE ENCHANTED WORLD
THE KODAK LIBRARY OF
 CREATIVE PHOTOGRAPHY
GREAT MEALS IN MINUTES
THE CIVIL WAR
PLANET EARTH
COLLECTOR'S LIBRARY OF THE CIVIL WAR
THE EPIC OF FLIGHT
THE GOOD COOK
WORLD WAR II
HOME REPAIR AND IMPROVEMENT
THE OLD WEST

This volume is one in a series of books describing countries of the world — their natural resources, peoples, histories, economies and governments.

For information on and a full description of any of the Time-Life Books series listed above, please write:
Reader Information
Time-Life Books
541 North Fairbanks Court
Chicago, Illinois 60611

COVER: A small 19th-century Catholic chapel nestles amid fir trees in Upper Bavaria.

FRONT AND BACK ENDPAPERS: A topographic map showing the major rivers, mountain ranges and other natural features of Germany appears on the front endpaper; the back endpaper shows the 11 states of West Germany and the 15 counties of East Germany, with principal towns and rivers.

Time-Life Books Inc.
is a wholly owned subsidiary of

TIME INCORPORATED

FOUNDER: Henry R. Luce 1898-1967

Editor-in-Chief: Henry Anatole Grunwald
Chairman and Chief Executive Officer: J. Richard Munro
President and Chief Operating Officer: N. J. Nicholas Jr.
Chairman of the Executive Committee: Ralph P. Davidson
Corporate Editor: Ray Cave
Executive Vice President, Books: Kelso F. Sutton
Vice President, Books: George Artandi

TIME-LIFE BOOKS INC.

EUROPEAN EDITOR: Kit van Tulleken
Design Director: Ed Skyner
Photography Director: Pamela Marke
Chief of Research: Vanessa Kramer
Chief Sub-editor: Ilse Gray

LIBRARY OF NATIONS

Series Editor: Tony Allan

Editorial Staff for *Germany*
Editor: John Cottrell
Deputy Editor: Ellen Galford
Researcher: Mark Karras
Designer: Lynne Brown
Sub-editor: Sally Rowland
Picture Coordinator: Peggy Tout
Editorial Assistant: Molly Oates

Special Contributors: The chapter texts were written by: Windsor Chorlton, Patricia Clough, Frederic V. Grunfeld, Alan Lothian, Mark Roseman and Margaret Wightman.
Other Contributors: Dr. Roger Morgan and Louise Earwaker

EDITORIAL PRODUCTION

Chief: Ellen Brush
Traffic Coordinators: Stephanie Lee, Jane Lillicrap
Editorial Department: Theresa John, Debra Lelliott, Sylvia Osborne

Valuable help was given in the preparation of this volume by Elisabeth Kraemer-Singh (Bonn) and Hans-Heinrich Wellmann (Hamburg).

Assistant Editor for the U.S. Edition: Karin Kinney

CONSULTANTS

Dr. Volker Berghahn is Professor of Modern History at the University of Warwick, Conventry. He has written several books and articles on 20th-century German history.

Patricia Clough is a former correspondent in Bonn for Reuters and, more recently, for the London *Times*.

Second printing. Revised 1987.

Printed in U.S.A.
Published simultaneously in Canada.
School and library distribution by Silver Burdett Company, Morristown, New Jersey.

TIME-LIFE is a trademark of Time Incorporated U.S.A.

Library of Congress Cataloguing in Publication Data
Main entry under title:
Germany.
  (Library of nations)
  Bibliography: p. 157
  Includes index.
  1. Germany. I. Time-Life Books. II Series: Library of Nations (Alexandria, Va.)
DD17.G47 1986   943   86-5766
ISBN 0-8094-5132-8
ISBN 0-8094-5305-3 (lib. bdg.)

PAGES 1 AND 2: The national emblems of the two Germanys are shown on page 1. The emblem of the Federal Republic has a black eagle with 10 feathers, a stylized version of the 12-feathered eagle adopted by the Holy Roman Empire of Germany and later by the Prussian-forged German empire of 1871 to 1918. The emblem of the Democratic Republic features a hammer and a pair of dividers, representing industry, and a wreath of ears of wheat, symbolizing agriculture. The two German flags *(page 2)* are fundamentally the same: a horizontal tricolor of black over red over yellow. The GDR, however, has its emblem at the center of the national colors.

CONTENTS

Sprawling on each side of the River Elbe, the city-state of Hamburg, with 1.6 million people, is West Germany's busiest port and second-largest metropolis.

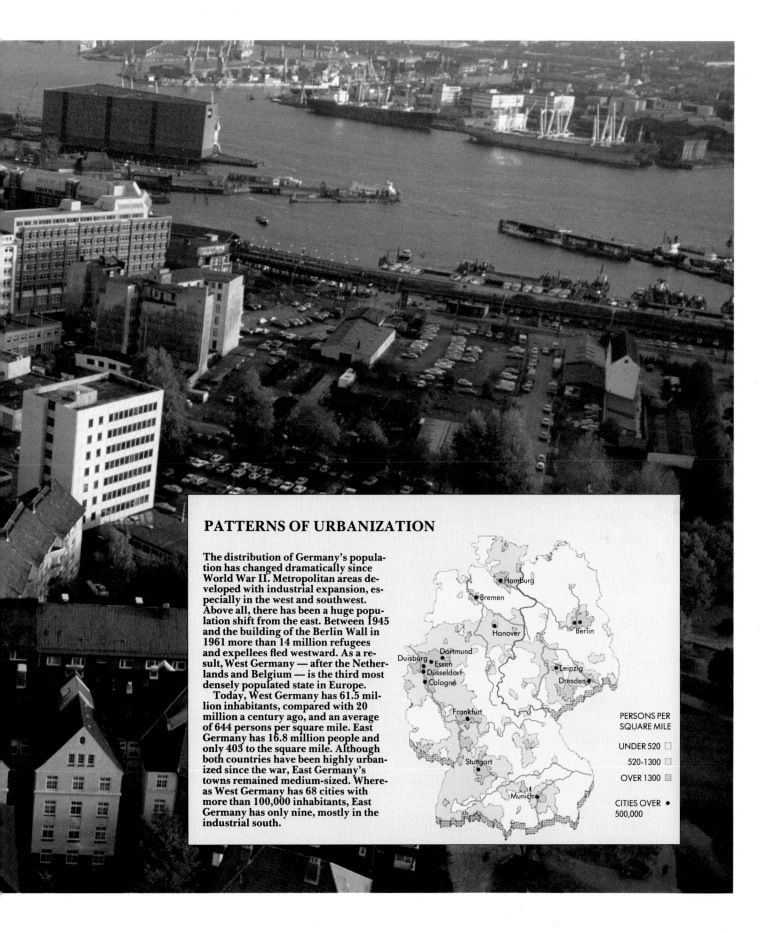

PATTERNS OF URBANIZATION

The distribution of Germany's population has changed dramatically since World War II. Metropolitan areas developed with industrial expansion, especially in the west and southwest. Above all, there has been a huge population shift from the east. Between 1945 and the building of the Berlin Wall in 1961 more than 14 million refugees and expellees fled westward. As a result, West Germany — after the Netherlands and Belgium — is the third most densely populated state in Europe.

Today, West Germany has 61.5 million inhabitants, compared with 20 million a century ago, and an average of 644 persons per square mile. East Germany has 16.8 million people and only 403 to the square mile. Although both countries have been highly urbanized since the war, East Germany's towns remained medium-sized. Whereas West Germany has 68 cities with more than 100,000 inhabitants, East Germany has only nine, mostly in the industrial south.

PERSONS PER
SQUARE MILE

UNDER 520 □

520–1300 □

OVER 1300 ▦

CITIES OVER ●
500,000

7

In the May Day parade, members of the Free German Youth stride through East Berlin beneath a blaze of flags bearing portraits of Communist heroes.

MOBILIZING THE COUNTRY'S YOUTH

There are approximately three million young people aged 14 to 25 in East Germany. More than three quarters of them belong to the Free German Youth (FDJ), a movement that developed out of antifascist youth committees formed immediately after World War II. Founded in 1946 by future head of state Erich Honecker, the FDJ now claims to have helped in raising and shaping almost half of East Germany's total population. The FDJ represents its 2.3 million members in all sectors of public life where their interests are at stake: in schools, colleges, collectives and factories. It also has 40 representatives in the 500-deputy People's Chamber, the East German parliament.

Through the FDJ, the energies and interests of East German youth are effectively harnessed. Members are organized into more than 6,500 youth clubs. They take part in German-Soviet festivals and in *Spartakiaden*, nationwide sports contests held biennially. They attend political rallies, and they take political classes to assimilate Marxism-Leninism and to become "convinced, class-conscious socialists."

As good socialists, FDJ members are encouraged to contribute directly to the economy by joining voluntary youth brigades formed to supplement the work force where urgently needed. In return for modest wages, such brigades help with a variety of projects — bringing in harvests, building dams, draining swamps, or working on joint German-Soviet enterprises, such as the recently completed Soviet pipeline that carries natural gas from Siberia to both Eastern and Western Europe.

DEEP-ROOTED TRADITIONS OF FAITH

In 1517, the north German monk Martin Luther launched a challenge to papal authority that culminated in the Reformation and the division of Germany into two warring camps, Catholic and Protestant. Today, in West Germany, the two churches are divided almost equally: about 26.7 million Catholics, largely in the Rhineland and Bavaria; and some 26.5 million Protestants, mainly in the north and east. However, only one third of the Catholics and less than 10 percent of the Protestants are regular churchgoers. In East Germany, where Protestants (some 7.7 million) far outnumber Cath-

olics (about 1.2 million), church attendance declined even more drastically. Only about 5 percent of East Germany's Protestants still go to church.

In the early 1930s, some 530,000 Jews made up Germany's most vital religious minority. Now, following the Nazi holocaust, there are only 28,000 Jews in West Germany, and about 1,500 in East Germany, half in East Berlin. Their numbers continue to decline while, in West Germany, a large religious minority increases: some 1.5 million Muslims, mainly Turkish "guest workers" and their families.

In the town of Chieming, in the predominantly Catholic state of Bavaria, girls in traditional dress walk to church for their first communion.

In a foundry in East Germany, white-hot steel is poured into a mold. East Germany ranks 10th among the steel-producing countries of Europe.

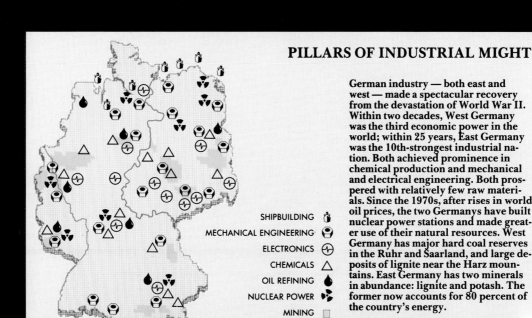

PILLARS OF INDUSTRIAL MIGHT

German industry — both east and west — made a spectacular recovery from the devastation of World War II. Within two decades, West Germany was the third economic power in the world; within 25 years, East Germany was the 10th-strongest industrial nation. Both achieved prominence in chemical production and mechanical and electrical engineering. Both prospered with relatively few raw materials. Since the 1970s, after rises in world oil prices, the two Germanys have built nuclear power stations and made greater use of their natural resources. West Germany has major hard coal reserves in the Ruhr and Saarland, and large deposits of lignite near the Harz mountains. East Germany has two minerals in abundance: lignite and potash. The former now accounts for 80 percent of the country's energy.

SHIPBUILDING

MECHANICAL ENGINEERING

ELECTRONICS

CHEMICALS

OIL REFINING

NUCLEAR POWER

MINING

PER CAPITA FOOD CONSUMPTION (POUNDS)

PREWAR GERMANY
EAST GERMANY
WEST GERMANY

320

240

160

80

0

MEAT   POTATOES   FLOUR   FRESH FRUIT   SUGAR

A CONSUMING LOVE OF FOOD AND DRINK

The German people — as first noted by the Roman historian, Tacitus — have always been renowned for prodigious appetites; and the reputation, as statistics show, is still merited. In recent years, however, there has been a swing away from such starchy staples as potatoes and flour, and a demand for fresh fruit and meat. The trend — a measure of German prosperity and greater diet-consciousness — has been most pronounced in West Germany. There, for example, the annual consumption of potatoes has fallen since prewar days from 387 pounds per capita to 176 pounds. In East Germany, the prewar figure has fallen to 310 pounds, but East Germany remains third — behind the Soviet Union and Poland — among the potato-growing nations of Europe. The low consumption of fresh fruit in East Germany is a reflection of supply rather than demand. When it comes to drink, Germans, east and west, retain their traditional place as the greatest beer drinkers. They are also drinking more wine, especially in West Germany, where consumption increased by almost half in the 1970s.

Fields of barley *(foreground)* and hops range over the rolling plains of lower Bavaria. West Germany is by far the biggest grower of hops in the world.

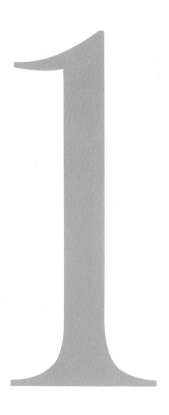

In their small East Berlin flat, a young
newspaper vendor and his student wife
breakfast with their family. To boost
the birth rate, East Germany gives
interest-free loans to couples who
marry before the age of 26. As children
are born, repayments are reduced; a
third baby cancels the debt.

money paid for major road and drain-
age improvements. Ironically, too, the
Iron Curtain ensured that Zicherie was
less isolated. A community so close to
the frontier became a curiosity — and
so, every year, many thousands of West
Germans drive from afar to see the
village that has fortifications across
its main street.

Zicherie has visibly prospered since
the war. Its nucleus of old red-brick
farmhouses is now fringed by a scatter-
ing of modern houses and bungalows,
all with potted plants and white lace
curtains in their windows. Every house
has modern kitchen appliances, color
television and good-quality furniture.
Each family owns at least one car —
most commonly a Volkswagen model.
In fact, it is to West Germany's gigantic
Volkswagen company that the inhabitants of Zicherie owe much of their

postwar prosperity. In 1938, the company established its headquarters at
Wolfsburg, 12 miles southwest of Zicherie and Böckwitz. After the war,
the Volkswagen factory achieved a
spectacular growth, and now about one
third of Zicherie's working population
is employed there.

For Böckwitz, the creation of the
east-west barrier has had the opposite
effect: The village, like other commu-

1

nities close to the eastern side of the frontier, has become both isolated and less prosperous because it is inside the 3-mile "forbidden zone," which no East German may enter without a special permit — and no Westerner may enter under any circumstances. Worse, the village falls mainly within the 1,650-foot "protective strip," where every movement of the populace is watched — if not by border guards, then by informers appointed by the authorities. Hence, security is so strict that no one may own a ladder without a special permit; and here a midnight curfew is permanently enforced, restricting late-night social activities and limiting outings to distant towns or villages. There is, of course, television; like most citizens of the GDR, people living within the restricted zone can readily tune in to West German channels. But this only serves as a telling reminder of the freedoms they are being denied.

Not surprisingly, according to some villagers in Zicherie, young people invariably move away from Böckwitz at the first opportunity. Now the village has fewer than 100 inhabitants, and most are elderly. They may possess small plots of land to grow fruit and vegetables for their own needs, but nowadays, if they wish to farm for a living, they need to join an agricultural cooperative. (Most agriculture holdings in the GDR were collectivized in 1959 and 1960. Now about 95 percent of the land is farmed by cooperatives, which total almost 4,000 and employ 92 percent of the country's farm workers.)

It is impossible to obtain a more detailed, firsthand picture of Böckwitz because no Westerner has access to the village. People in Zicherie can see friends living at the other end of their main street only by arranging a rendez-vous somewhere in East Germany, at least 3 miles beyond the border. They must make a long detour, driving nearly 24 miles south to the nearest of the nine highway crossings between the Federal Republic and East Germany; then, when they arrive, there are the tedious formalities of the border to be faced.

Over the years, the polarized positions of the two German countries have become clearly defined. West Germany, a country with a total area of 99,452 square miles (including the 192 square miles of West Berlin) and divided into 11 federal states (Länder), is a self-governing republic firmly integrated into the Western political and socio-economic systems. It is a full member of the North Atlantic Treaty Organization (NATO) and of the European Economic Community (EEC), and it has a form of democratic government that combines elements of American federalism and of the British parliamentary system. East Germany, which covers 43,333 square miles and is divided into 15 counties (Bezirke), is a Communist state forming part of the Soviet bloc. It is a member of the Warsaw Treaty Organization and of the Council for Mutual Economic Assistance (Comecon), and it has a Soviet-style system of government.

In West Germany, elections for all legislative bodies are general, direct and secret, and every citizen who has attained the age of 18 is eligible for a vote and is free to stand as a parliamentary candidate. The labor laws recognize that the workers have the right to engage in free collective bargaining and that trade-union members can call strikes if necessary. In East Germany, political power is permanently held by

In the fertile countryside of northern Bavaria, the Wörnitz River winds placidly past russet-roofed farmhouses set among fields of oats and barley. The mixed crops and narrow fields typify the traditional small-scale farming that survives in West Germany.

the 2.2-million-member Socialist Unity Party (SED) or, to be more precise, by the 25 leading members of the SED who make up the Politburo, a self-perpetuating body whose decisions influence every aspect of life in East Germany. There is no legal opposition; and the constitution no longer states, as in its original 1949 version, that citizens have "the right to strike" and "the right to emigrate."

The West German economy is based on the principle of the free "social market" economy that was introduced in 1948 under the auspices of the Western Allies. This system, operating under the tenet of "as little state as possible, as much state as necessary," tries to promote individual economic initiative in a competitive market, and at the same time rejects the social injustices of 19th-century *laissez-faire* capitalism and the inflexibility and authoritarianism of the state-planned economy. By statutory means, the government is able to curb practices and agreements — for example, cartels and syndicates — that are liable to influence market conditions by restricting competition. However, a few key enterprises — most notably the German Federal Post Office and German Federal Railways — are in public ownership; agriculture is heavily subsidized and, like other sectors of the economy, subject to the regulations governing the EEC.

In East Germany, market forces of supply and demand are not allowed to dictate volume of production and prices. All major industries and enterprises are nationalized; and the GDR operates a fully centralized and planned economy in which the state, as directed by the Socialist Unity Party, has total control of the means of production and distribution. To a large ex-

tent, the state planners allocate scarce resources, decide on many production priorities, set long-term growth objectives, control prices, and even fix profit levels and investment patterns for the individual industries and plants.

Thus, in almost every way, the political and socioeconomic philosophies of the two Germanys are diametrically opposed. Indeed, East and West Germany take fundamentally different views of how they relate to each other. Contrary to the GDR attitude, the Federal Republic officially recognizes that Germans — whether living in the east or in the west — are still one people forming a single nation. Although both East and West Germany are independently members of the United Nations, the latter still does not recognize the former as a separate nation. It maintains its viewpoint that there is only one Germany: a nation composed of two sovereign states.

In *Facts about Germany*, a government publication widely distributed abroad, the West German attitude is expressed as follows: "Almost 40 percent of the inhabitants of the Federal Republic have relatives or acquaintances in the GDR; leading Federal German politicians were born in what is now GDR

territory, leading GDR politicians in what is now the Federal Republic. This is a degree of personal intertwinement that can rarely occur between alien nations. But, above all, the inhabitants of both the Federal Republic and the GDR continue to feel as members of one German nation, linked by a common language and history and many other common heritages which cannot simply be wiped away from one day to the next."

Guided by this attitude, West Germany refuses to recognize East Germany as a foreign country in terms of international law; and this gives rise to a number of peculiarities in the relationship between the two Germanys. For example, the Federal Republic imposes no import duty on products coming from the GDR and charges mail going to East Germany at the domestic postal rate. There are no exchange rates between the currencies of the two German states. Furthermore, West Germany does not have a constitution. Instead it has a *Grundgesetz* (Basic Law), a term chosen in 1949 when it was felt that a definitive constitution should not be written until the reunification of Germany. The last article of the Basic Law states explicitly: "This Basic Law

On a cooperative farm in East Germany's southwest *(left)*, women plant tree seedlings; a bulletin board *(below)* praises the skills of two of the co-op members. Women run one in three of East Germany's 4,000 agricultural cooperatives and make up 42 percent of the farming and forestry work force.

FRAUEN AUF DER TECHNIK

shall cease to be in force on the day on which a constitution adopted by a free decision of the German people comes into force."

In keeping with this lingering hope, successive West German governments have persisted in recognizing June 17 as the Day of German Unity, a public holiday commemorating the anniversary of the brief uprising in East Germany against Communist rule in 1953. That day, construction workers in East Berlin protested against higher work norms decreed by the government, and their action touched off strikes in many other cities of the GDR as workers expressed their disapproval of the regime. In East Berlin, demonstrations were suppressed by Soviet tanks; 21 demonstrators died and many more were injured. Officially, West Germans celebrate the anniversary as proof of the undying determination of all Germans to achieve reunification. But in reality, most West Germans see no real purpose in the celebrations — a fact reflected a few years ago in a poll that showed more than 70 percent of the population of the Federal Republic believed that formal unity with East Germany was no longer possible.

This has become an inescapable con-clusion in the light of the GDR's official attitude toward reunification. Original-ly, East Germany's constitution de-scribed the country as a "socialist state of the German nation." But not any more. Now, in the words of its revised (1974) constitution, it is "a socialist state of workers and peasants," and it is "for-ever and irrevocably allied with the Union of Soviet Socialist Republics."

The majority of East Germans natu-rally feel closer to the people of West Germany than to any of their non-German-speaking Warsaw Pact allies and neighbors. Moreover, several mil-lion East Germans have friends and rel-atives in the Federal Republic. But the GDR leadership takes the view that there can be no real bridge between capitalism and socialism, and that peo-ple living under such opposite social systems must develop entirely different values and a different consciousness. It therefore stresses the differences between East and West Germany, re-jects any notions of a reunified nation and discourages east-west contacts by travel restrictions.

West Berliners are allowed to spend no more than 45 days a year in the Ger-many that surrounds them. This is a restriction imposed by the GDR leader-ship to underline its objections to West Berlin's far-reaching integration into the legal, economic and social systems of West Germany. The official GDR view is that West Berlin, still technically governed by Britain, France and the United States, is an "independent po-litical unit" devoid of any ties with the West German state.

All other citizens of the Federal Re-public are permitted to visit East Ger-many as often, and for as long, as they wish. But the cost of this privilege is high. There is a charge for each visa issued, also a tax on motorists for "the use of East German roads" — a charge that seems harsh, since the Federal Re-public has contributed millions of Deutsche Marks toward the construc-tion and improvement of *Autobahn* links with Berlin. The West German government, seeking to encourage con-tact between the two Germanys, foots the bill for the car tax. But, in addition to paying for a visa, the individual trav-eler still has the burden of excessive currency exchange rates. Every day, any Western visitor who is not staying at an East German hotel must change a fixed amount into East German cur-rency. The West Germans get only one GDR mark for one Deutsche Mark (DM), compared with an unofficial ex-change rate of at least four-for-one on the black market, and money changed cannot be reconverted or taken out of East Germany.

Significantly, in October 1980, the East German government tripled the currency exchange demand to a mini-mum of DM 25 per day. By this means, they maintained the level of income de-rived from West German visitors and at the same time achieved a 40 percent re-duction in the number of Westerners visiting friends and relatives in the east.

VILLAGE WAYS IN THE INDUSTRIAL HEARTLAND

Garden plots of the Eisenheim suburb form an oasis of greenery amid Oberhausen's industry.

Father and son wheel home a load of cabbages grown on their garden plot.

The Ruhr is the industrial heartland of West Germany. Its cities form one vast, sprawling metropolitan area sometimes called *Ruhrstadt* (Ruhr City); and here some four million people are crowded together, many housed in high-rise buildings that overlook a gray and sooty world of coal mines, foundries, rolling mills and blast furnaces that belch smoke clouds by day and inflame the sky at night. Yet, remarkably, in this industrial inferno, thousands of workers still enjoy a semirural lifestyle — growing their own vegetables, keeping livestock, and generally preserving the close-knit atmosphere of a village.

One such community is the Eisenheim miners' colony in the industrial city of Oberhausen. Here, some 140 families live cheek-by-jowl with coking plants and blast furnaces. They live in 39 two-story buildings built between 1844 and 1901. Behind these homes, on family garden plots, miners grow produce and keep goats, chickens, rabbits and pigs. Twice a year, a butcher slaughters pigs, and the meat is stored in family freezers.

Eisenheim is the oldest of more than 1,000 colonies established in the Ruhr in the 19th century by coal-mining companies to house their workers. Its traditional way of life was threatened in 1958 when the landlords planned to replace the dwellings with 10- and 15-story buildings. But the miners campaigned for two decades, and

in the late 1970s, they won protection for their urban village under the Historic Buildings and Monuments Act; the authorities agreed to modernize their homes. Since then, other mining communities have been encouraged to fight high-rises and so maintain pockets of country life within the engine room of the German economy.

A butcher guts a pig on a biannual visit to the urban village.

From an attic window, a retired miner keeps an eye on his pigeons.

Eisenheim residents relax in a social center, originally washhouses.

The pragmatism of the GDR leadership is made still more obvious in the ruling that allows only East Germans of retirement age — 65 for men and 60 for women — complete freedom to visit the west. These privileged citizens are no longer of value to the GDR; and if they should choose to stay permanently in West Germany, the GDR is then instantly relieved of the onus of providing their pensions.

Every year West Germans manage to register more than eight million visits to East Germany. However, excluding retirees, fewer than 50,000 East Germans annually are able to obtain permission to travel west. They are privileged businessmen, trade-union officials and prominent party members, or else ordinary citizens who can prove they have special personal reasons for making a private visit to West Germany — for example, to attend a silver wedding anniversary party, or a confirmation or funeral of a blood relation. In contrast, East German pensioners make more than 1.5 million visits to West Germany every year — an incredibly high figure considering that the total number of pensioners in the GDR is approximately 3.2 million. So it is that one of the jokes in West Germany describes East Germany as the one country in the world where people can look forward to growing old.

Over the years East Germans have displayed extraordinary courage and ingenuity in their attempts to reach the west. Freedom-seekers have escaped across the border by tunneling, swimming, and hiding in the chassis of motor vehicles; by hijacked railroad train, by breeches buoy and by tightrope walking over the Berlin Wall; even by hiding in a stuffed and mounted cow

AN ALLIANCE OF STATE AND PARTY

East Germany is not, officially, a single-party state: Five political parties, allied with trade unions and other mass organizations, work toward a socialist society. But within this coalition — known as the National Front — the Socialist Unity Party (SED) is the dominant force. Its hegemony is enshrined in the country's constitution, which affirms that the state is "led by the working class and its Marxist-Leninist party."

Every workplace has its SED unit. From this base, activists may join local and regional organizations and serve as delegates to the Party Congress, which meets every five years to elect the Central Committee — usually 25 members. Real power, however, lodges with the Secretariat in charge of the party bureaucracy. Its head, the general secretary, is also the leader of the Politburo. This élite, about 25 senior party officials, ministers and military officers, is the source and arbiter of public policy.

Every tier of government — from the municipal parliament, looking after village affairs, to the People's Chamber, passing laws for the nation — is dominated by SED members. At elections, there is a single list of official candidates, compiled by the National Front, that includes a token number from the minority parties. Participation in the democratic process is zealously encouraged, and about 98 percent of the electorate does vote.

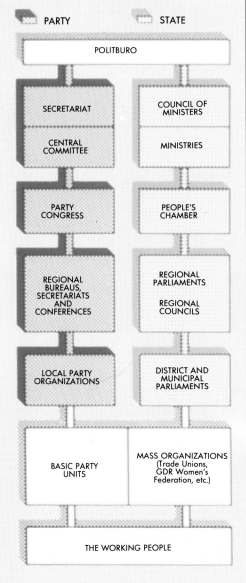

on its way to a West German dairy show. Especially remarkable was the successful escape in 1979 of two couples, the Strelzyks and the Wetzels, each with two children. In September of that year — shortly before the start of the celebrations for the 30th anniversary of East Germany — they crossed the "impenetrable" frontier at a height of 8,250 feet, riding in a colossal, multicolored, homemade hot-air balloon, to land near Naila, a small town in West Germany, 12 miles west of Hof in northern Bavaria.

That flight from the East German town of Pössneck covered 24 miles and lasted no more than 28 minutes. But it was the culmination of a year and a half of nerve-racking endeavor — planning, gathering materials, building, rebuilding, contriving in secret to test-fly two balloons, each larger than a four-story house, and once landing inside the 3-mile "forbidden zone," amid woods lined with trip-wire trigger devices. Their decision to escape was noteworthy, too, because both families were well-to-do in East Germany, each pos-

sessing their own home, automobile and all basic household furnishings, each with their future secure. Yet they chose to sacrifice it all in exchange for a life in the west.

Long ago, in the light of such daring escapes, West Germans had a wry saying that roughly translates: "If the government ever demolishes its east-west barriers you had better climb a tree — otherwise you will be trampled to death in the rush." The saying had obvious validity in the desperate years following the building of the Berlin Wall, when

A COHESIVE FEDERATION OF STATES

FEDERAL PRESIDENT

DIRECTLY ELECTED

NOT DIRECTLY ELECTED

CHANCELLOR

FEDERAL GOVERNMENT

BUNDESTAG

FEDERAL CONVENTION

BUNDESRAT

LAND PARLIAMENTS

LAND ADMINISTRATIONS

ELECTORATE

COUNTY AND MUNICIPAL PARLIAMENTS

West Germany is a federal republic, a union of 11 separate, internally self-governing states (Länder), each with its own elected parliament and administration. Within this system, citizens' interests are represented in two ways: through 520 deputies directly elected to the *Bundestag*, the nation's parliament and, indirectly, through the *Bundesrat* (federal council), comprising 45 delegates appointed by the governments of the states themselves.

The delegates of the *Bundestag* plus an equal number of delegates sent by the state parliaments form the federal convention, which elects the federal president. The president's powers are largely symbolic: He ratifies government appointments, signs treaties and represents West Germany abroad. Real political power rests with the federal chancellor. Elected by the *Bundestag* for a four-year term, he directs federal policy and proposes the ministers responsible for turning these policies into action.

In a delicatessen on East Berlin's Alexanderplatz, shoppers pause before a lavish array of meats and sausages. This well-stocked store, part of a new shopping complex, is government-controlled — and caters only to service personnel, government officials and Eastern-bloc tourists.

every year thousands risked their lives in seeking to follow the 2.7 million East Germans who had crossed to West Germany between 1949 and 1961. But nowadays, when there are less than 1,000 people escaping in any one year, it is not so certain that the removal of the Iron Curtain would trigger a mass stampede westward.

Of course, it can be argued that the number of escapes from East Germany is much lower because the security measures have become more sophisticated since 1961. Only 1 percent of refugees now choose to escape by way of the Berlin Wall or the border death-strip; the rest flee by more devious means — for example, via another East European country while there on vacation, or perhaps by seeking political asylum in the west after convincing the GDR authorities that they can be trusted to visit West Germany privately, or as a member of some overseas trade delegation or sports team. Logically too, it may be argued that the very existence of the Berlin Wall and the death-strip is proof enough that the GDR government still fears the possibility of a mass exodus to the west.

Nevertheless, there are good reasons for believing that a large, indeterminable number of East Germans have come to accept life in a Communist Germany. As a West German journalist observed a few years ago after working as a correspondent in the GDR: "Sometimes we forget that the majority of the 17 million people living in East Germany have come to terms with the regimented political and social system governing them. Most of them have accepted the German Democratic Republic as their home — just as it is, in spite of its imperfections."

But there is more to it than that. A

great number of East Germans — irrespective of their political beliefs — take positive pride in belonging to a country that, with a relatively small population, has managed to become the second-greatest industrial power (after the Soviet Union) in the Eastern bloc and, even more astonishingly, the strongest sporting nation, per capita, in the world. East Germany first established its sporting supremacy at the 1976 Olympic Games in Montreal by winning more medals than any other participating country except the Soviet Union, which has a population 16 times as large as the GDR's. Remarkably, it even managed to outscore the United States, whose population is 14 times the size of the GDR's.

It is significant, too, that there is now emerging a second generation of East Germans who have never experienced life in a non-Communist environment,

and who, like the generation before them, are systematically taught to appreciate the principles and benefits of Marxism-Leninism. To be sure, they are well informed about the way of life in the west via West German television, which the majority of East Germans can, and do, watch regularly. They see a Germany offering greater freedom and higher living standards. But they also see a more permissive, violent, materialistic and competitive society where the wealth of the nation is less evenly divided among its inhabitants and where ordinary citizens are continually exposed to the twin perils that go with a free market economy: inflation and unemployment.

At the same time, of course, many East Germans see plenty to criticize in their own country: the much-loathed restrictions on travel abroad; the constant political pressures in everyday life; the frequent shortages arising in a thousand and one things, from fresh vegetables and imported fruits to safety pins and ballpoint pens; the poor quality of many consumer goods; the long wait for certain "luxuries" — for example, 10 years or more for the delivery of a new car; the innumerable perks and privileges accorded Communist party functionaries in a professedly egalitarian society.

Still, the fact remains that East Germans enjoy the highest living standards in the entire Communist world — including the Soviet Union. As in the Federal Republic, almost all households have a television set, a refrigerator and a washing machine. Only 37 percent of households own a private car, compared with 62 percent in West Germany; however, this represents a huge advance over the 1970 figure of 16 percent and compares very favorably with Russia's 13 percent. Since 1960 the monthly average wage for all households has risen 100 percent, to 1,500 marks.

In the meantime, by way of vast government subsidies, the cost of many basic necessities has remained unchanged. These include potatoes, milk and rye bread — all much cheaper than in West Germany. The price of a streetcar ticket — one mark for a journey of any length — has not risen since the 1940s. Tickets for the theater, movies and sports events sell at prices established 20 years ago.

This stability in the value of the mark has been a major plus for the economy in the eyes of the East German population, among whom, until recent years, there were many who remembered the terrifying German inflation of 1923. But there are snags in government price-fixing. While the cost of certain

basic items has not risen in decades, the cost of many other items long ago classified as "luxuries" — for example, electrical gadgets, coffee, chocolates and imported fruits — has not fallen since the GDR was founded. For decades, coffee has remained hugely expensive at 32 marks a pound — roughly a third of the cost of a new bicycle. Moreover, while there is no private enterprise and competition to encourage price-cutting, there are frequent shortages of goods that enable prices to be pushed up on a flourishing black market.

With the advantages of a common language and the mutual window of television, the German people, east and west, are in a unique position to see close up the many differences between everyday life under communism and capitalism. Comparing the two Germanys is a fascinating exercise and one that many Germans find irresistible. Overall, however, comparative facts and figures prove only that the socioeconomic systems of both Germanys have their advantages and disadvantages, and that ultimately the choice between them rests on personal and political values.

Meanwhile, year by year, the inhabitants of the two Germanys become more deeply entrenched in their positions and therefore grow further apart. They are still discernibly the same people: They possess the same tongue, though no longer the same second language (these days it is Russian for East Germans and English for West Germans), the same cultural heritage, and many of the same tastes and traditions. They can relate closely to one another as individuals. But the societies in which they live, and the power blocs to which they are bound, remain fundamentally incompatible. □

A West German guard surveys the bogs and ditches of Jardelunder Moor, a desolate stretch of the Federal Republic's frontier with Denmark.

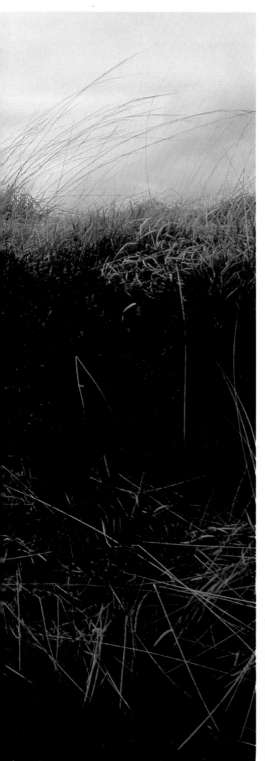

A WATCH ON NINE FRONTIERS

Photographs by Frieder Blickle

Along its 2,550-mile perimeter, the Federal Republic of Germany shares frontiers with nine countries. No other state in Europe has as many foreign neighbors on its periphery; no nation of comparable size has so many different boundaries to control. Some 6,700 armed customs officers, with 1,250 trained dogs, guard the land and water margins of West Germany, and some 20,000 border police patrol the fortified East German frontier. Security is made more onerous by the extraordinary variety of the terrain. West German frontiers run along Alpine ridges, through dense forests and bog-ridden moorland, across lakes and rivers, sometimes dividing villages, farms and even houses. Officials must patrol in all weathers—on skis in mountain blizzards, by boat during spring floods. On the other hand, most boundaries they survey are friendly; indeed, with neighboring Switzerland, Austria and Luxembourg, cordial relations are further enhanced by the bond of a common language.

Heraldic shields representing Austria and Germany decorate a mailbox located in a mountain inn, high in the Bavarian Alps. The German-Austrian border runs directly through the inn, and the proprietor has to split his taxes evenly between the two governments.

The longest West German frontier is the 829-mile border with East Germany; the shortest is the 41 miles abutting Denmark. The only natural boundaries lie south, where the Alps, Lake Constance and the Rhine separate West Germany from Austria, Switzerland and France.

During the floods that frequently submerge the German-French frontier on the banks of the Rhine, white daubs on trees serve as temporary border markers to guide two German customs officers to their customs house, near Karlsruhe. These officials control the access of water-borne traffic into West Germany by boarding barges to examine their cargoes; smaller craft have to dock at the house for inspection.

At the border village of Lichtenbusch, near the ancient city of Aachen, two officials — a Belgian *(left)* and a German *(right)* — look out from the windows of their shared customs house, which straddles the frontier.

Near the ditch that divides his farm into West German and Danish land, a German farmer shows the passport that allows him access to both sides. A postwar boundary agreement left him his house and 95 acres of land in the Federal Republic; his cattle graze on 27.5 acres in Denmark.

Celebrating their annual festival, bandsmen of a West German gun club parade across the Dutch border that traverses the village of Suderwick. People of two nations — separated only by a boom across the main street — share a hospital, fire station and each other's stores and inns.

On her way to Sunday service, a German churchgoer approaches a bridge linking West Germany with the Grand Duchy of Luxembourg. Across the bridge is the only place of worship in this rural region — a Catholic church in Untereisenbach that serves both sides of the border.

Within view of a customs hut and landing pier, a wind surfer glides over Lake Constance, which separates Germany and Switzerland. Swimmers and pleasure craft may cross over the 27-mile-long border, but anyone landing on either side is subject to passport and customs controls.

At the popular West German beach resort of Priwall, in Lübeck Bay, East German floats extend the east-west border 330 feet into the Baltic, warning swimmers not to stray out of bounds in these heavily patrolled waters.

Ostensibly, only a fence and a sign-post mark this stretch of the Bavarian border with Czechoslovakia. But some 330 feet inside the Czech territory, behind the trees, are electric fences and watchtowers. In contrast, the West German side is so open that Czech cows often stray onto its soil.

Bearing a boundary marker emblazoned with the emblem of the Federal Republic, a customs officer treks up the 5,610-foot-high Kreuzkopf ridge, which divides West Germany and Austria. In this Alpine region, local officials spend much of their time replacing boundary signs lost in blizzards and avalanches.

As morning breaks over the Möncke-bergstrasse, a main artery of Hamburg, the city comes alive with rush-hour traffic. West Germany is one of the world's most heavily urbanized nations; one in three of its citizens lives in a large town or city.

the building of the 59-mile Kiel Canal, a shortcut across Schleswig-Holstein that spared ships a 450-mile voyage around the northern tip of Denmark to reach the Baltic from the North Sea; construction of the Mittelland (Middle-land) Canal to provide a 195-mile link between the Ruhr and Berlin; and various projects that led to the development of the most important waterway in Europe — the 792-mile-long Rhine, and its tributaries, the Neckar, Main, Moselle and Ruhr. Then, in the 1930s, Germany built Europe's first highways, which, like the waterways, have been continually improved and extended since World War II.

Today, West Germany's *Autobahnen* constitute the busiest and longest highway system in Europe, linking all major industrial centers and providing key international routes. This is also one of the fastest highway networks in the world: West Germany (the land of Karl Benz, who designed and built the first gasoline-powered automobile in 1885) has chosen not to have a speed limit. Some Germans drive on the highways at speeds approaching 150 mph, and the average is about 78 mph — at which speed motorists can travel the full length of West Germany (512 miles) in about 10 hours, and its breadth (135 miles at the narrowest point) in roughly two hours. Such enormously increased mobility encourages people to commute greater distances to work, and it generally makes the Federal Republic seem a far smaller place.

West Germany is one of the most densely populated lands in the world, with 624 inhabitants per square mile, as opposed to 403 inhabitants in the GDR. Consequently it has very few areas that remain completely untouched by hu-

45

Silhouetted in the twilight, harborside cranes and a television tower dominate the Hamburg skyline. At Germany's busiest port, equipped with the most advanced information technology, ships dock, offload their cargo and depart in a matter of hours.

man settlement or activity. To be sure, there are great tracts of forest; the country is almost the same size as Britain, and yet 29 percent (18 million acres) of its land is forested compared with only 8.5 percent (4.75 million acres) in Britain. But even the largest wooded areas — the *Schwarzwald* (Black Forest) in the southwest, the *Bayerischer Wald* near the Czechoslovak border, and the Harz Mountains straddling the east-west frontier — are under the supervision of regiments of forest rangers and are crisscrossed with clearly defined and well-marked pathways.

Beyond these forests, Germany as a whole is dotted with thousands of small villages and sprawling urban centers that are separated by plowed fields and grasslands used mainly for dairy farming. More than 60 percent of the land is taken up by agriculture. Yet, despite the predominance of forest and farmland, few stretches of topographical monotony are to be found. One is in the north along the barren, windswept North Sea coast. Another is in Lower

Saxony, where flat rye fields and fenced-in grasslands stretch as far as the eye can see and then give way in the east to the Lüneburg Heath, a haunting region of heather-covered moorland punctuated by juniper trees, birch woods, rocks and fields of *Heidschnucken* (moorland sheep) grazing near timber-framed farmhouses.

Germany can be divided into three main topographical zones that stretch from west to east: the North German Plain (Lowlands), the Central Uplands, and the Alpine Foreland in the south. The Lowlands, a mainly flat region about 96 miles wide in the west and much broader in the east, embrace the West German states of Schleswig-Holstein, Hamburg and Bremen, most of Lower Saxony, the northwest of North-Rhine Westphalia and about three quarters of East Germany, that is to say virtually all GDR territory north of a line drawn horizontally through the cities of Leipzig and Dresden. The Uplands, a vast area composed largely of high plains and undulating hills and valleys, range across southwest and central West Germany and the southern counties of the GDR. The Alpine Foreland, a wide, gently sloping region roughly bordered by the Danube in the north and the Alps in the south, extends over the southeast of Baden-Württemberg and Upper Bavaria.

Thus, Germany slopes steadily upward from north to south — from the Lowlands, where the land rarely rises above 495 feet, to the Alpine fringe crowned by Germany's highest mountain, the 9,775-foot Zugspitze. As a result, with the notable exception of the Danube, most of the land's rivers and their tributaries flow northward and exit into the North Sea or the Baltic.

On the West German side of the

Lowlands, commerce and industry thrive around the main ports — the largest being Hamburg on the lower reaches of the Elbe, Bremen near the estuary of the Weser, and Lübeck on the River Trave, 8 miles from the Baltic Sea. But elsewhere, this region — so sandy and loamy and exposed to the elements — is ill-suited to supporting a substantial population. The land lies almost imperceptibly above the sea; indeed, along the North Sea coast, there are no cliffs — only wide expanses of sand, marsh or mud flats.

The division between rural and urban dwellers is most pronounced in this part of the Federal Republic. More than six centuries ago, north German cities and German commercial groups abroad founded an association (the Hanseatic League) to promote and safeguard their mutual trading interests. As a result, Hanseatic cities on the Baltic and North Sea developed into great seafaring and trading centers — rich, proud and fiercely independent. Through their links with the outside world, the people of these cities became the most cosmopolitan of Germans.

Foreign influence shows most in Hamburg, a great seaport that, despite heavy bombing during World War II, maintains traditionally strong ties with Britain. Some of its suburbs, with their spacious villas and gardens, are reminiscent of wealthy residential areas in the so-called "stockbroker belt" south of London. Here, people may be seen wearing British-style blazers and flannels, tweeds and tartans, and a visitor may hear citizens complaining of the "English weather."

Hamburg is now the fourth-largest seaport in Europe and the most populous West German city, excluding isolated West Berlin. Bremen, the Federal

NORTH SEA

BALTIC SEA

HAMBURG

ROSTOCK

BERLIN •

• ESSEN

• BONN

LEIPZIG •

FRANKFURT •

• STUTTGART

MUNICH •

- NORTH GERMAN PLAIN
- CENTRAL UPLANDS
- ALPINE FORELAND

The German land mass slopes upward in a southerly direction through the flatlands of the north, the rolling terrain of the central belt and the towering ridges of the Alps. As the altitude rises, the climate changes: Winters are often coldest, and summers shortest, in the southern part of the country.

Republic's second-largest seaport and only other city-state, could never rival Hamburg's importance because the Weser, unlike the Elbe, is not deep enough to take the largest ships. Instead, these ships must dock about 36 miles northwest, at Bremerhaven, strategically well placed at the mouth of the Weser, and now a major passenger port and shipbuilding center as well as West Germany's foremost fishing center, accounting for some 50 percent of all landings.

Strongly contrasting with the Lowlands' worldly, sophisticated Hamburgians are the taciturn Frisians, whose way of life is likely to be fishing, farming or dairying. The Frisians live on the islands along the North Sea coast and on the shores of Lower Saxony and Schleswig-Holstein. Over the years, they have been made the target of endless jokes by other Germans, who mischievously choose to portray them as archetypical country folk unable to come to grips with modern technology.

In turn, and more justifiably, the Frisians find much amusement — or rather wonder — in the way so many Germans pay good money every summer to visit North Sea resorts and spend weeks acquiring a wind-driven suntan and braving the cold, pounding surf. For centuries these proud and rugged people have lived with the wind and sea as their enemies. They have toiled to reclaim land for farming and have struggled to protect their lands by building dikes and great chains of shifting sand dunes. Yet, time and again, the sea has surged back, destroying their homes, flooding their fields and sometimes permanently changing the map.

The Lowlands on the GDR side are distinctly different. Here, myriad shallow lakes, great and small, are scattered across a region bounded by the Baltic in the north. There is only one great seaport, Rostock, which, like Bremerhaven in the west, is also an important fishing and shipbuilding center. Before changes in Germany's boundaries after World War II, this area had no major harbor; it was served principally by Hamburg and Stettin. Now Hamburg is in West Germany and Stettin is in Poland, and consequently new harbors have been built — besides Rostock, at Warnemünde, Wismar and Stralsund. None, of course, gives the GDR easy access to the North Sea — one of East Germany's great losses as a result of the east-west frontier being established just 30 miles east of Hamburg.

In the east, unlike the west, the largest and most important city of the Lowlands is inland: Berlin, the sundered metropolis that began life as a 12th-century fishing village on the banks of the River Spree and emerged some 700 years later as the first capital of a united Germany. The development of Berlin has been truly remarkable considering that it was built in a region of great marshes and on flat, low-lying land that was known as "the sandbox of the Holy Roman Empire." Even now, when foundations are deeply laid, the digging equipment comes up with the purest golden sand. And southeast of the city, in the region of Spreewald, the land is so swampy that outdoor life is lived largely in flat-bottomed boats, and houses and haystacks are built on stilts to keep them out of the dampness.

Although sited 108 miles from the sea, Berlin began to prosper in the 17th century because it proved a vital link in the network of overland trade routes that led from more southerly towns such as Meissen and Dresden to the Baltic coast, and from Magdeburg in the west to the ancient Polish city of Cracow and the territories of Russia in the east. Now, ironically, the western half of Berlin is absurdly ill-placed in terms of trade. It is a major industrial center of the Federal Republic, without free and direct access to a hinterland in which to sell its products; an exclave without its own corridor, the nearest West German point on the *Autobahn* being at Helmstedt, 100 miles away.

HOSTAGES TO THE TIDES

About 1 mile off the coast of the West German state of Schleswig-Holstein lies a cluster of tiny islands known as *Halligen,* or holms, part of the North Frisian archipelago. The 400 inhabitants earn their livelihoods mainly from tourism and cattle-farming, but their way of life is dominated by the unpredictability of the sea.

Houses, barns and cowsheds are built only on the highest ground, because an island, such as Gröde-Appelland, that is green and tranquil in the summer months *(above)* may be all but swallowed up by the waves during winter floods *(right).* During this season, storms buffet the islands, and the sea level rises.

The descendants of Dutch settlers who migrated to the islands in the Middle Ages have lost half of their territory to the sea in the last 300 years. In recent years, an extensive system of walls and dikes has largely arrested this attrition. But the sea still reigns supreme and, in the words of an old Frisian motto, "Joy and sorrow come and go like the ebb and flow."

Snow-covered conifers line the banks of the River Ammer in Bavaria. Forests — mostly spruce and pine — cover nearly one third of the Federal Republic. But Germany's sylvan landscapes are now under threat from industrial pollutants falling as acid rain and gradually poisoning the soil.

In contrast, East Berlin, capital and largest city of the GDR, is ideally placed to be the hub of its country's political and economic life.

The Central Uplands form Germany's largest topographical zone and embrace the most varied landscape: mountains, valleys, forests, farmlands and great industrial complexes. In the Federal Republic, the zone ranges over the tiny state of Saarland, rich in coal; parts of Lower Saxony and North-Rhine Westphalia; and the state of Rhineland-Palatinate, including the most spectacular stretch of the Rhine (between Koblenz and Bingen), where the tourist discovers that those almost impossibly romantic postcard pictures of Rhineland castles and islands, villages and gorges do not exaggerate. It also covers all of the largely agricultural state of Hesse, a rolling patchwork of dark woods alternating with brown and green fields set on hills gently sloping down to picturesque villages and river valleys. This is territory rich in folklore — the land of the brothers Jacob and Wilhelm Grimm, those supreme 19th-century reapers of fairy tales, who settled in Berlin and devoted years to compiling the definitive German dictionary, a work so comprehensive and detailed that neither brother lived to see progress beyond the letter *F*.

In eastern Hesse, the Central Uplands rise into the Harz Mountains, a region of gray, pine-clad hills, dramatic gorges and sleepy villages that spans the border with the GDR. Beyond these mountains, in the far southeast of the GDR, the industrial powerhouse of East Germany lies within a triangle formed by the *Bezirke* (counties) of Leipzig, Dresden and Karl-Marx-Stadt. These counties — named like all others after their most important cities — are the three most densely populated in East Germany. Karl-Marx-Stadt heads the list with a population of 1.9 million and a density of 832 inhabitants to the square mile. More than 50 percent of the county's work force is engaged in industry, most notably mechanical engineering, vehicle manufacture and textile production.

West Germany's counterpart — roughly on the same parallel — is the Ruhr district, an area of approximately 1,600 square miles where about 9 percent of the West German population lives on only 2 percent of its territory, so producing a density of about 3,640 inhabitants per square mile. Here, at the heart of North-Rhine Westphalia, sprawling industrial cities — Dortmund, Bochum, Essen, Duisburg, Düsseldorf and Cologne — merge almost imperceptibly and embrace a constellation of smaller towns to form a vast urban mass sometimes referred to as *Ruhrstadt* (Ruhr City).

More commonly, the Ruhr has been known for decades as the *Kohlenpott*, the "coal bowl." In this bowl, a huge concentration of mine shafts, chimney stacks, furnaces and factories, and grimy, multistory apartment complexes rise alongside 19th-century miners' cottages and rows of terraced houses. Yet, somehow, the countryside never seems far distant. Visitors are often surprised to see through the indus-

trial haze and smog a herd of cows ruminating in a field; and the proximity of fields and factories is even more striking in the hilly, wooded area south of the River Ruhr and in the Wupper River valley, where the textile and iron production of Germany's industrial revolution flourished in 19th-century family workshops, and where Friedrich Engels, friend and collaborator of Karl Marx, worked before he moved to England.

North-Rhine Westphalia is the most industrialized and most populated of *Länder*. Yet the Westphalian part of the state is deeply agricultural. Indeed, because of the state's mixture of industry and farming, the population is said to reflect almost exactly the social make-up of West Germany as a whole, and so it is often the hunting ground of pollsters and market researchers. Just to the south, in the neighboring *Land* of Rhineland-Palatinate, another industrial complex runs along the Rhine south of the state capital, Mainz, and in Hesse along the Main River, south of Frankfurt. Great chemical factories, oil refineries and automobile plants, and high-technology companies form the backbone of these areas. Here, again, one straggling town merges into another; however, new highways have encouraged workers to commute from suburban or rural areas rather than live in heavily built-up urban districts, as in the older towns of the Ruhr.

All these great industrial complexes of the western Uplands have, of course, one huge advantage over those in the east: ready access to the Rhine and its tributaries. Rising in the Swiss Alps and flowing to the North Sea, the Rhine is navigable to barges larger than 2,000 tons as far as Rheinfelden, east of Basle, Switzerland, at the extreme southwest

corner of the Federal Republic. The great barges handle about three quarters of all of West Germany's waterways freight, which totals at least 250 million tons a year — mainly gravel, sand, timber, fuel oil, coal and iron ore. And Duisburg port, at its confluence with the Ruhr, has become the world's largest inland port system and the second busiest (after Hamburg) in Germany.

The Rhine divides Rhineland-Palatinate from another highly industrialized state on its southeastern side. This is Baden-Württemberg, a state boasting many ultramodern industries, among them the great Mercedes automobile plant and the large electronics and car-component factories around the state capital, Stuttgart. It is the fastest growing *Land* of the Federal Republic, and not surprisingly so since this region is the traditional home of the Swabians, a people renowned for their industry and thrift. The Swabians' motto, in dialect, is *Schaffe, schaffe, Häusle baue* (Work hard, work hard, and build a little house). They also have another telltale saying: *Hund verkaufe, selber belle* (Sell your dog and do your own barking). Like their cousins across the Swiss border, the Swabians are shrewd at business, but their shrewdness and industry tend to be tempered with a sunny nature and an abiding love of the countryside.

Baden-Württemberg is well geared to combine industry with an appreciation of outdoor life. Indeed, it prides itself on being the *Musterländle*, the "little model state," because its enormous industrial growth has been achieved without detracting from its beautiful countryside: the vineyards of Baden stretching down to the Rhine, the rocky Schwäbische Alb mountains near the Danube and, most notably, the Black

2

Forest, so named for the dark giant fir trees that set off the emerald green of its lush valleys and the silver of its lakes.

Beyond the Danube, to the southeast, Baden-Württemberg lies within the Alpine Foreland, the southernmost topographical band, which, though bordered by the mighty Zugspitze, is mainly composed of accessible peaks, together with forests, lakes, deep valleys and numerous small villages highlighted by brightly painted farmhouses and churches with onion-shaped steeples. The Foreland also embraces the southern half of Bavaria, the largest state of the Federal Republic; and it vies with the Rhineland as the region best known to tourists.

Directly north of the Zugspitze lies the village of Oberammergau, famed for its Passion Play, first held in 1634 to give thanks for deliverance from the plague, and now staged in the first year of each new decade. And 9 miles west of Oberammergau, perched high on a steep, barely accessible crag, is another great tourist attraction: Castle Neuschwanstein, one of the wildly ornate, fantasy creations of Bavaria's "mad" King Ludwig II, 19th-century benefactor of Richard Wagner.

Here begins the famous *Romantische Strasse*, the "romantic road," that extends some 210 miles north through a wonderland of turreted castles, towering cathedrals and ancient walled towns seemingly unchanged since the Middle Ages. The highway crosses the Danube just north of the 2,000-year-old city of Augsburg and ends at Würzburg, where the sumptuous Bishop's Palace boasts one of the largest paintings in the world: Tiepolo's *Four Continents of the Earth,* a medley of allegorical figures that covers the 6,512 square feet of the

palace's vaulted ceiling. And east of Würzburg, Bavaria has yet another cluster of ancient towns steeped in romance: Bamberg with its medieval cathedral; Bayreuth, resting place of Wagner and Liszt; and Coburg, with its 16th-century fortress, 9 miles from the border with East Germany.

Bavaria is not all farming country interspersed with dreamy spires and quaint towns and villages. It has built up a considerable industry, mainly composed of small and medium-size enterprises. Nuremberg, some 90 miles north of the state capital, Munich, has a long-established high-technology and toy industry, and its satellite city of Erlangen is the center of the Siemens electronics trust, West Germany's largest private company. However, Bavaria has the most extensive areas of farmland (9.25 million acres) in West Germany, and is the most rural, religious and tradition-conscious of *Länder*.

Bavarians, who have close affinities with neighboring Austria, tend to be earthy, jovial and ruggedly individualistic. Some north Germans would describe them less flatteringly; in the great game of interregional sniping, it is not unusual for the Bavarians to be caricatured as overindulgent, loudmouthed pleasure-seekers totally lacking in refinement. But Bavarians do not give a fig for what other Germans think of them. *Mir san mir* (We are us) they say; in other words, take us as we are. Supremely proud of their origins, they cannot forget that Bavaria was once prosperous and well governed, and they feel themselves just that little bit more separate, that little bit more different, from other Germans.

Bavarian pride is so assertive that visitors may feel they are entering an independent country as they cross over

from Hesse or Baden-Württemberg and confront signs in white and blue (the colors of the ancient House of Wittelsbach, which ruled from 1180 to 1918) proclaiming the "Free State of Bavaria." The individuality of Bavaria is also exemplified by its own intense form of politics. The conservative Christian Democratic Union (CDU), which has long been the principal rival of the Social Democratic Party (SDP) for national leadership, exists in every West German state except Bavaria. The independent Bavarians choose to have their own version of the CDU: the Christian Social Union (CSU), which has been in coalition with its big sister, the CDU, since 1947.

In the 1950s, the CSU began to develop into a major political force under Franz Josef Strauss, an ebullient, energetic and eloquent embodiment of all things Bavarian. Germans outside Bavaria were sometimes shocked by Strauss's more eccentric political ideas, his forceful, highly colored language, his explosive temperament and habit of shooting verbally from the hip. But Bavarians loved his style. He was their Franz Josef, a true son of Bavaria, putting other Germans in order.

In 1972 Willy Brandt, then Federal Chancellor, hurled the supreme insult at Strauss when he called him the "last Prussian from Bavaria." Historically, no two German states have detested each other more than Bavaria and Prussia. Today Prussia no longer exists; after World War II, East Prussia was divided and placed separately under Polish and Soviet administration, and the rest of Prussia was distributed among 11 of the 17 *Länder* then existing within the four zones of occupation. Nevertheless, one may still hear Bavarians using the old, familiar term of

providing facilities for the children of working mothers. In the GDR, more than 60 percent of children younger than three are left in day-care centers operated by the state, and more than 90 percent of children from three to six years old have places in state-run kindergartens. These facilities are vital to the country's ability to fully utilize its potential work force.

According to government statistics, 87 percent of East German women of working age from 16 to 60 have a job outside the home. This is as it should be in a country whose constitution states that it is the duty as well as the right of every citizen to work. Of course, this high percentage is not unconnected with the fact that wages are relatively low and that the attainment of a comfortable standard of living depends on the earning power of both the male and the female partner. Nevertheless, it is not to be denied that the GDR is managing to perform an extraordinary double act: maintaining a huge female work force while encouraging its citizens to boost the population.

Until 1973, the GDR birth rate — like that of the Federal Republic — was steadily falling. Since then, however, it has steadily risen — from 10.6 to 14.4 births per 1,000 inhabitants every year — while the annual death rate has averaged 13.9 deaths per 1,000 inhabitants. Thus, unlike West Germany, the GDR is now maintaining a fairly static population level, with the number of births almost equaling the total number of citizens lost each year by death and by legal or illegal departure to the west. At the same time, however, as the result of a rigidly state-controlled socioeconomic system, it is undeniably developing into a Germany that is far less rich in variety and contrasts. □

In the heart of Munich, the floodlit façade of the 19th-century *Siegestor* (Victory Arch) dominates the Leopoldstrasse. Every year Munich draws millions of tourists, making it the fourth most visited city in Europe, after London, Paris and Rome.

THE SPIRIT OF BERLIN

Berlin is Europe's most extraordinary city. Divided by a concrete wall nearly 15 feet high, it encompasses within its 335 square miles two diametrically opposed political systems. East Berlin, capital of East Germany and 1.1 million people strong, is one of the most prosperous socialist metropolises in the world. West Berlin, with 1.9 million inhabitants, is the largest West German city, yet it lies 100 miles inside East Germany, surviving as an isolated city-state with its own forests, lakes and farmland—all enclosed within the fortified perimeter of the Berlin Wall.

East and west, Berliners have always prided themselves on being different from other Germans. They have their own dialect, their own sardonic humor, and their own indomitable spirit, which has sustained them through war, dictatorship and foreign occupation. Berliners consider themselves more cultured, progressive and cosmopolitan than their compatriots—perhaps because their city has always been an international crossroad, a magnet for creative, rebellious spirits, drawn here by the highly charged atmosphere that Berliners themselves call the *Berliner Luft,* the heady Berlin air.

As a legacy of World War II, Berlin is divided into four parts. In 1945, each of the victorious Allies took control of one section of the city. The western part of the city comprises the French, British and American sectors; East Berlin is the Soviet zone.

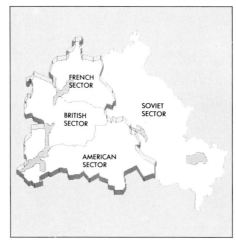

Decorated with whimsical paintings and graffiti, a section of the Berlin Wall provides the backdrop for a children's ball game in West Berlin. The wall cuts resolutely across city streets and suburban gardens as well as rural fields and forests.

Watched by his foreman, a worker repairs sewage pipes in West Berlin's Charlottenburg district. Most of the west's sewage is piped to treatment plants in East Berlin and the surrounding countryside. Municipal rubbish, too, is transported through a gate in the wall to dumps in the east.

Poised on top of a brick chimney in East Berlin, a chimney sweep hauls up his weighted cleaning brush, releasing a cloud of dust from the flue. The top hat, badge of his trade, proclaims his status as a journeyman in the chimney sweeps' guild. Chimney sweeps are a familiar sight on both sides of the city.

In a West Berlin street, a deliveryman (below) steadies a load of coal briquets. The fragile blocks of pressed coal, widely used in the stove fires and ovens that still heat many Berlin homes, are liable to disintegrate unless packed individually in wooden racks.

A WORKING DAY IN THE CITY

A fisherman from the East Berlin Fishing Cooperative unloads a catch on Grosser Müggelsee, one of the 13 lakes within the city limits of East Berlin. The city incorporates 110 miles of waterways, providing abundant pike, perch and whitefish, and the eels that are prized as a local delicacy.

In a field fringed by suburban highrise buildings, just outside the city center, a West Berlin farmer harvests his wheat. More than 100 farms, occupying 7.5 percent of West Berlin's total land area, grow enough wheat and barley to meet the city's needs.

High-rise apartments, sharply outlined against the sky, are a familiar sight on both sides of the city. Complexes such as these West Berlin buildings are gradually replacing the 60 percent of Berlin's housing destroyed during World War II, but there is still a serious housing shortage, east and west.

A young squatter gazes from the window of his temporary home in Kreuzberg, West Berlin's most densely populated district. Because developers find it cheaper to build new units than to renovate existing buildings, some 7,000 apartments in the west stand empty or are occupied by squatters.

HIGH-RISES AND TENEMENTS

An elderly East Berliner sits on her doorstep in Prenzlauer Berg, an inner-city borough whose 19th-century tenements were heavily damaged in wartime bombings. In this district alone, the state renovates 500 apartments a year, but — as in the west — many thousands of homes are not yet modernized.

In the center of East Berlin, a gigantic statue of Lenin guards the entrance to a modern high-rise complex of apartments. The authorities allocate housing according to the greatest need, giving priority to families with children.

ENJOYING THE OPEN SPACES

The shadow of the Winged Victory monument falls across West Berlin's Tiergarten. Once an 18th-century deer reserve, this magnificent park was replanted after wartime bombing.

Replete after their feast, picnickers loll under trees on the banks of the Grosser Müggelsee. Extensive woodlands and spacious municipal campsites make it possible for East Berliners to enjoy a day off in the countryside without leaving the city.

Scantily clad or completely nude, sunbathers crowd a park near the center of West Berlin. Even in their own densely populated city, Berliners happily tolerate nudism — a movement that started in Germany in the early years of the century.

Honoring an old custom, East Berlin newlyweds set off for their reception in a horse-drawn carriage with a top-hatted driver. Despite their traditional dress, the two were married in the city hall. Notwithstanding the official atheism of East Germany, more and more people have a church wedding.

A llama from West Berlin's zoo inspects a passerby's donation to an animal-welfare charity. The zoo — one of the largest of its kind in Europe — frequently lends out exotic animals to help raise funds for worthy causes.

Passersby on Kurfürstendamm pause to watch actors posing as marble statues at the beginning of a skit. Street entertainers of all kinds — musicians, snake charmers, mime artists and clowns — have turned this West Berlin boulevard into an outdoor theater.

STREET THEATER

A posse of West Berlin cowboys, representing the Old Texas Cowboy Club, attract only mild attention from café patrons. Members of the club, one of many in West Germany, don costumes to raise money for charity.

In the ornate surroundings of the Café Haus Q'Dam, Berliners enjoy a leisurely chat. For patrons of such traditional establishments, rich cakes, accompanied by coffee or a *Berliner Weisse mit Schuss* — white beer injected with a dash of raspberry syrup — is a much-loved daily ritual.

Youthful patrons crowd the bar of the Café Abax. Since the 1960s, West Berlin has experienced a steady influx of young people, drawn by the city's vibrant cultural and social life.

A chorus line of transvestite dancers
performs in a West Berlin nightclub.
Such cabarets have been a Berlin
trademark since the 1920s, giving the
city its lasting reputation for
decadence, daring, and an easy
tolerance of alternative lifestyles.

Rich merchants and a busy harbor represent prosperity in an illustration from Hamburg's Municipal Code of 1497. As members of a powerful consortium, the Hanseatic League, German ports enjoyed a virtual monopoly over North Sea and Baltic trade in the 15th and 16th centuries.

CENTURIES OF CONFLICT

"This country is open to all the winds of the continent," said André François-Poncet, French ambassador to Germany before and after World War II. And therein lies one of the keys to Germany's turbulent history of wars, upheavals, and centuries of disunity. It stands at the crossroads of Europe, traversed by the great, predominantly flat North German plain. Only the sea to the north and the Alps to the south provide natural frontiers. And the country's seven major rivers — the Rhine, Ems, Weser, Elbe, Main, Oder and Danube — have historically served more as aids than obstacles to the free movement of people. Such a land was destined from the beginning to attract nomads, colonists and invaders.

Archeological evidence has been able to establish that German territory was inhabited at least 50,000 years ago by Neanderthals, sturdy predecessors of modern humans. Neanderthals are named after the place where the first fossil remains of this forebear were found in 1856 — a cavernous limestone ravine in the Neander Valley near Düsseldorf. Many additional Neanderthal skeletons were found later in Europe, Africa and Asia, and the original skull is now a prized exhibit in the Rhineland Museum in Bonn.

At the time of that first discovery, diggings at Hallstatt, in upper Austria, were revealing a wealth of information about Celtic tribes who had inhabited much of the central European plain, from present-day Hungary to Brittany, in the late Bronze Age and early Iron Age — approximately 3,000 years ago. There, in a prehistoric cemetery and salt mine, excavations unearthed evidence of a civilization that was incredibly rich in works of art. Between 1846 and 1899, more than 2,000 graves were uncovered. Because of the preservative nature of salt, the bodies of Celtic miners had remained intact — together with an astonishing array of decorated bronze shields, helmets and drinking vessels, iron swords, gold jewelry and finely crafted pottery.

Between the end of the Bronze Age and the second century B.C., these Celtic peoples were gradually displaced by Teutonic, or Germanic, tribes migrating into the German plain from the north and the east. The invaders made their first appearance in written history in 113 B.C. when two of the tribes, the Cimbri and the Teutones, defeated a Roman army near Noreia in Carinthia, in the Eastern Alps. In turn, however, they were later annihilated by a great punitive force commanded by the renowned Roman general Marius.

In 58 B.C. Gaius Julius Caesar launched his conquest of Gaul, and in three years he had subjugated those Germanic people who had settled on Gallic territory west of the Rhine. Roman legions later marched north along the Rhine and colonized the area that now makes up the westernmost *Länder* of the Federal Republic. But when the Romans sought to expand their empire eastward, from the Rhine to the Elbe, they suffered a terrible defeat by Germanic forces led by Hermann, a chieftain of the Cherusci tribe.

Hermann (more commonly known by his Latin name, Arminius) had been taken to Rome in his youth, probably as a hostage, and there he had studied Latin and Roman military history. How diligently he studied was evident in 9 A.D., when he led an uprising that vanquished three Roman legions (about 20,000 men) in the hilly region of the Teutoburg Forest, south of modern-day Bielefeld. Centuries later, he came to be recognized as the first German national hero, and he is now commemorated by a colossal monument situated high on a mountain near Detmold, not far from the ruins of an old Germanic fort.

The Romans, accustomed to doing battle on open ground and in well-ordered formations, were much less formidable in dense forests, fighting enemies adept at hand-to-hand combat. Therefore, after brief retaliatory campaigns, they chose to limit their colonization to the open lands along the Rhine and the Danube. Between the headwaters of the two rivers they built defenses, some 330 miles long, to secure their territory against incursions from the east.

At the end of the first century A.D., the Roman consul and historian Tacitus wrote the first extensive account of the fierce, independent peoples who lived beyond the frontier and who were known in Latin as the *Germani* (possibly from a Celtic word meaning "the shouters"). His *Treatise on the Situation, Manners and People of Germania* — though tinged with the prejudice of a colonist — is indispensable as an anthropological report on the Germans at the

3

beginning of their history. He recorded that they comprised many different tribes, some of them sedentary and some nomadic. They were a proud, frank and generous people, though Tacitus formed the opinion that their intrepid warriors became listless sluggards in time of peace, or else they sought out other tribes who had some war in hand that they could join: "For the Germans have no taste for peace; renown is more easily won among perils, and a large body of retainers cannot be kept together except by means of violence and war."

When the German warriors marched into battle, they shouted a blood-curdling war chant, and they moved in groups of families and clans, with the women and children following close behind "so they can hear the shrieks of their womenfolk and the wailing of their children." The warriors wanted to perform deeds of valor for the women, for it was they who would later "count and compare the gashes." Moreover, he observed, some German armies had been "rallied by the women, pleading heroically with their men, thrusting forward their bared bosoms and making them realize the imminent prospect of enslavement — a fate the Germans fear more desperately for their women than for themselves."

Tacitus judged that the Germans, for all their pagan superstition and warrior tradition, were a remarkably law-abiding people; above all, he praised their respect for marriage as a strict and sacred institution. Only virgins could marry, and widows, no matter how young and beautiful, were forbidden to take a second husband. Adultery was extremely rare — and with good reason. When detected, the punishment was instant and inflicted by the husband. "He cuts off her hair, strips her naked, and in the presence of kinsmen turns her out of his house and flogs her all through the village. They have in fact no mercy for a wife who prostitutes her chastity. Neither beauty, youth, nor wealth can find her a husband." No one in Germany, Tacitus stressed in his treatise, found vice an amusing subject — a far cry from the mores of ancient Rome.

For the greater part of the first and second centuries A.D., the Romans maintained peaceful relations with the German peoples; and they established a number of important towns, most notably Augsburg, Bonn, Cologne and Trier. But then the numerous Germanic tribes began to regroup and larger, more powerful tribes emerged, among them the Alemanni, Burgundians, Franks, Frisii, Goths, Lombards, Saxons, Suevi and Vandals. The Romans, with their overstretched lines of communication, had more and more difficulty in keeping these formidable tribes at bay. Finally, during the fourth and fifth centuries, the frontier defenses gave way. The Goths, Burgundians, Franks, Vandals and other tribes poured across the Rhine River, along with some newcomers — the ferocious Huns, who had stormed across Germany from Asia.

Attila and his Huns inspired fear throughout Europe. But after Attila's death in 453, his many sons fought among themselves and consequently the great empire of the Huns disintegrated, its survivors fleeing back east, beyond the Volga. Of the many tribes that remained in Germany, the Franks were by far the most powerful. King Clovis, the first great Frankish leader, who reigned from 481 to 511, made Paris his capital and established the

A modern sketch of a first-century relief details a village plundered by Roman soldiers. The Romans never totally subjugated the Germans, and the historian Tacitus confessed: "Neither by the Samnites nor by the Carthaginians, not by Spain nor Gaul, have we had more lessons taught us."

Merovingian dynasty, which ruled for two and a half centuries over a feudal kingdom consisting of virtually all of France, the Low Countries and western and southern Germany.

In the eighth century, the Merovingians were supplanted by the Carolingian dynasty, so named by modern historians after its most celebrated son, Charlemagne (Carolus Magnus), or Karl der Grosse as he is known to German history. Charlemagne, king of the Franks from 768 to 814, extended his empire over most of Western Europe and eventually established his court in the German town of Aachen, just west of Cologne, where his bones rest to this day. Statesman, lawgiver and military strategist, he was dubbed *rex pater Europae* — king father of Europe — by a poet at his court. Equally, he may be regarded as the father of Germany. He was responsible, by way of long, savagely waged wars, for the conquest of the pagan Saxons and their conversion to Christianity; and during his reign, the great German tribes — Alemanni, Bavarians, Saxons and Thuringians — were gathered for the first time into one political unit.

In Rome, on Christmas Day, 800, Pope Leo III crowned Charlemagne as Roman Emperor — the Christian ruler of an empire that comprised present-day West Germany, Austria, western Czechoslovakia, northern Italy, Switzerland, France and the Low Countries. Some 40 years later, after the death of Louis the Pious — Charlemagne's last surviving son — this empire was divided among three heirs. It became three separate kingdoms arranged along a north-south axis, and so the precious heritage of a united Europe was lost. Nonetheless, rulers of the emerging German kingdom in the east continued to see themselves as the sole heirs to Charlemagne, and in the 10th century they revived the custom of going to Rome to receive the imperial crown from the Pope's hand.

The tradition was to lead to the complex, far-reaching concept of the Holy Roman Empire of the German Nation and to the grand imperial illusion that the German emperors had inherited both the power of the Caesars and the glory of the universal church, and were therefore the feudal overlords of other kings and princes, deriving their authority from God.

These Roman Emperors ruled over an empire, or *Reich*, that consisted of only Germany and northern Italy; their title notwithstanding, they exercised no power over Rome itself. Even inside Germany the emperor's authority was often disregarded by his vassals; here,

In an illumination from a 14th-century manuscript, Charlemagne, emperor of the western Roman Empire from 800 to 814, receives his crown. A militant defender of the faith, Charlemagne brought the last of Germany's pagan tribes into the Christian fold.

3

he was no more than the head of a loose confederation of feudal princes. Yet the German lords continued to regard the Holy Roman Emperor as their legitimizing authority for any honors and distinctions; the emperor invested princes with their principalities, issued the letters patent that could grant a city its "freedom" or a soldier his knighthood, and so directly contributed to the fragmentation of Germany.

In the middle of the 12th century, the empire came under the brilliant rule of Frederick I, surnamed Barbarossa on account of his fiery beard. Barbarossa was the foremost of the Hohenstaufen emperors and the model medieval ruler: "A magnificent, magnanimous man," as Thomas Carlyle described him, "holding the reins of the world, not quite in the imaginary sense; scourging anarchy down and urging noble effort up, really on a grand scale." In his 38-year reign, he encouraged the growth of towns, the development of Bremen, Hamburg and Lübeck as important maritime trading centers, and the extension of German power over the former Slavonic territories to the east. He raised Austria to the status of a duchy (previously it had been ruled by a mere margrave) and asserted his imperial authority over Bohemia, Poland and Hungary.

In Italy, however, Barbarossa became embroiled in a long and bloody series of campaigns against the papal power of Rome; and at home he struggled in vain to curb the ever increasing power of rival German princes. Whereas France, during his lifetime, developed into a centralized monarchical state, Germany became more deeply entrenched in a system of independent territorial states. Centuries later, German romantics would glorify Barbarossa as a symbol of national unity, but in truth, after his death the consolidation of a single German nation-state was more remote than ever.

Barbarossa died in 1190, accidentally drowning in a Turkish river while on the Third Crusade. His body was never recovered, and so a legend arose that he lived in a cavern deep in the Kyffhäuser mountain in Thuringia, awaiting the moment when his country would recall him to the throne. Actually, the Hohenstaufen emperors were to lose their hold on Germany in trying to become the masters of Italy. After the last of their dynasty was beheaded in 1254, Germany was racked by two decades of chaos and civil war. The Holy Roman Empire of the German Nation had become a legal fiction.

Meanwhile, the Middle Ages had produced a magnificent body of literature in the two forms of the language that are called Old High German and Middle High German. The lords and ladies of the German courts were spellbound by brilliant poets, including Wolfram von Eschenbach, author of the 25,000-line epic *Parsifal* — the tale of the "guileless fool" who embarks upon the quest for the Holy Grail and eventually acquires wisdom. Another supremely poetic picture of German court life was provided by Gottfried von Strassburg's *Tristan and Isolde,* an uncompleted epic of nearly 20,000 lines that was to become one of the enduring love stories of world literature.

But the courtly tradition that sustained this burst of literary creativity was already on the wane when the great Hohenstaufen dynasty came to an end. During this period of decline and disintegration, there was open warfare between the great feudal princes, and local lords often became robber barons.

It was the merchants and craftsmen of the emerging cities — the burghers of the walled towns — whose fortunes rose while those of the nobles were falling into disarray. They managed to establish great trade associations, of which the Hanseatic League was by far the most powerful — a union of maritime and inland cities for the purpose of encouraging trade, safeguarding trade routes on sea or land, and regulating the conditions of commerce among merchants in various corners of Europe. The League's activities centered on the city of Lübeck and the Baltic Sea, but extended as far as Russia, Scandinavia, England and Spain.

As trade increased, Germany entered a period of economic growth, but it was a prosperity in which the overwhelming majority of German people had no share. By 1500, Germany was still a predominantly rural society. There were only 15 cities with a population of 10,000 or more, the largest being Augsburg with some 50,000. Of an estimated population of 12 million, approximately 10.5 million lived off the land. The peasants ended up with higher taxes and reduced rights, and their sole legal recourse was to the manorial court, where their grievances were almost always dismissed or ignored.

Beyond the safety of the well-ordered towns, the prevailing pattern was one of continuous strife and civil disorder. Germany was divided into more than 300 separate duchies, principalities, countships, bishoprics and self-governing cities, all of them disposed to use armed incursions by bands of mercenaries as a means of settling their local disputes.

The Hapsburgs of Austria now held the imperial crown more or less as a family monopoly. Yet they found they

were unable to impose their authority on this checkered assortment of states.

Though the emperor still retained great prestige, in practice he now ruled only Austria, Bohemia and Hungary — a complex of polyglot kingdoms whose interests diverged increasingly from those of such German states as Bavaria, Saxony and Brandenburg. From this time forward, Austrian history was to develop along distinctly separate lines from those of its neighbors to the west and the north. Meanwhile, the latter had only their language in common, and even this presented difficulties. Dialects varied so much from one region to another that the Low Germans of the coastal areas had trouble understanding the Swabians, and the Rhinelanders were bemused by the German spoken by Saxons or Brandenburgers.

The great noble families alternately fought or supported the Hapsburgs and engaged in sporadic wars against one another, while at the same time the self-governing cities fought the nobles and the ecclesiastical princes. These autonomous cities conducted their own foreign policy; sometimes they had to go to war against a neighboring bishop or archbishop who might press his claims to local sovereignty, not in the name of church or emperor, but as yet another independent power, acting on his own initiative.

This political confusion was further compounded by the Protestant Reformation. When the strong-willed monk and theologian Martin Luther challenged the authority of the Pope in 1517 by tacking his 95 theses to the church door in Wittenberg, Saxony, he began a process that was to end in the division of the whole of Germany into two warring camps, Catholic and Protestant. On the face of it, the Reformation was concerned with theological issues, but the movement also had a social and economic dimension. The prosperous trading cities and commer-

PIONEER OF THE PRINTED WORD

"The invention of printing is the greatest event in history, the mother of all revolutions," said Victor Hugo. The genius who sparked this revolution (far left) was Johann Gutenberg of Mainz (1397-1468).

Until the invention of printing, books were hand-copied. To achieve mass production, Gutenberg devised quickly made metal letter type, an efficient press, oil-based ink and cheap rag paper.

In 1455, after seven years' work, Gutenberg produced his first printed book — a bible (sample page, left) in an edition of 200 copies. By this time, he was hopelessly in debt, and his principal creditor took over the press and established the first firm of printers and publishers.

In a woodcut entitled *The Difference between the True Religion of Christ and the False Ungodliness of the Antichrist,* the Protestant artist Lukas Cranach the Elder (1472-1553) contrasts Luther's reformed Christianity with the corruption rampant in the church of Rome. On the left, Protestants worship the God of love and listen to Luther preaching; on the other side, the God of wrath sends down fire and brimstone on a blighted land where clerics sell pardons to sinners and pervert the sacraments, and a demon in a bishop's miter sits on the shoulder of a leering priest.

cial states of northern Germany were the most receptive to the new teachings and most eager to rebel against pope and emperor. In Saxony and Hesse, the struggle between the old faith and the new thus concealed a contest between the traditional feudal order and the emerging middle classes.

The downtrodden peasants also responded to the spirit of the times and began to resist attempts by the feudal lords to exploit them still further. In 1524, the Peasants' Revolt erupted in the Black Forest; it spread during the next year through southern Germany (excluding Bavaria), Hesse, Thuringia, Saxony and Tirol. The peasants adopted as their battle cry Luther's plea for "liberty of Christian men," but they only aroused Luther's wrath when their rampaging included the destruction of ecclesiastical establishments. In the absence of any real leadership or strategy, the peasants suffered appalling loss of life inflicted by the armies of territorial princes, and those who survived were taxed more heavily than ever by way of reparation.

Bavaria, the Catholic bastion in the south, at first played only a marginal role in the doctrinal conflict inspired by Luther. When Duke Albrecht V came to the throne of Bavaria in 1550, he pursued a policy of cautious neutrality in the ongoing wars between the Catholic Hapsburgs and the league of Protestant princes headed by the ruler of Saxony. His ministers rightly suspected him of being lukewarm in matters of religion: Clearly his real passion was reserved for music, art and all the sundry pleasures of court life. He ran up vast debts in order to build private museums such as the *Antiquarium* and *Kunstkammer,* which he stocked with Roman antiquities and Italian Renaissance paintings and sculptures that were purchased for him by his agents in Rome, Venice and Mantua.

Albrecht's patronage of the arts was so great that it might have sparked a literary and artistic renaissance in Germany comparable to the humanist revival that had taken place elsewhere in Europe, producing such figures as Shakespeare, Tasso and Montaigne. But the incipient German renaissance was nipped in the bud by the increasing violence and intolerance demonstrated by Catholics and Protestants in the great religious divide.

In the latter period of his reign, Albrecht himself abandoned his policy of toleration toward dissenters. All those who persisted in the Lutheran heresy would henceforth be banished from the duchy, although this judgment meant losing many of the most prosperous craftsmen and merchants of Munich, who promptly migrated to Protestant cities farther north. When the Munich city council complained that this exodus was costing them 100,000 florins a year in lost taxes, Albrecht replied that his subjects' spiritual salvation mattered more than money and that he could not tolerate heretics in his own capital. Thus the stage was set for yet another painful confrontation in the steadily widening rift between formerly peaceful neighbors.

Similar outbreaks of bigotry were taking place throughout central Europe. By 1618 these tensions and provocations erupted into one of the most violent and destructive of all European conflicts, the Thirty Years' War. It began as a Bohemian Protestant revolt against Roman Catholic rule and eventually spread to involve most of the countries of Western Europe. During the next three decades Ger-

3

many was turned into a killing ground where plundering armies, led by generals who were interested only in self-aggrandizement, terrorized the civilian population. Religious principles counted for very little indeed, since generals and whole armies could reverse allegiances and march off to fight on the side of the highest bidder.

By the time the war ended, with the Peace of Westphalia — a treaty that took four years to negotiate — neither the Protestant nor the Catholic states of Germany had sufficient strength to dominate the nation. The result was a compromise: The treaty stipulated, "There shall be an exact and reciprocal equality among all the electors, princes and states of both religions — all violence and force between the two parties being forever prohibited." In contrast, most other European countries emerged from the Thirty Years' War with clearly defined religious majorities — Protestantism in Britain, the Netherlands and Sweden, Catholicism in France, Italy and Austria.

The Thirty Years' War represents the low point of German history. The nation's population was reduced from approximately 21 million to 13.5 million. Thousands of towns and tens of thousands of villages and castles were totally destroyed, and in some communities the local population was reduced to cannibalism. Furthermore, in concluding the Peace of Westphalia, the great powers purposefully preserved the fragmentation of Germany by recognizing more than 300 German states as sovereign entities.

Thus the German renaissance to which Albrecht V aspired in the mid-16th century never blossomed into full glory. Its only important literary monument is Martin Luther's translation of the Bible, from Hebrew and Greek into German. This work was largely responsible for giving Germany a literary language, in the same way that the King James version of the Bible has left an indelible stamp on all subsequent English and American prose.

In the 17th century, once the smoke of war had finally lifted, Germany embarked on a long and impressive period of physical reconstruction and cultural ferment. The burgeoning baroque age produced many outstanding architects, as well as a spate of fascinating writers, scholars and musicians: for example, the author Grimmelshausen, whose novel *Simplicius Simplicissimus* exposed the brutalities and absurdities of the just-concluded war; Leibniz, the mathematician and philosopher who theorized about the first principles of matter; and perhaps the most significant of all, Johann Sebastian Bach.

Bach's music, with its daring modulations and breathtaking counterpoints, is always unmistakably his own, but at the same time it sums up the *genius loci* of baroque Germany, with its logic, rationality, piety and imagination. His relationship to the epoch, however, was

In this 16th-century German woodcut, half-naked provincial knights (small landholders) are in savage conflict with their exploitive overlords in a battle of the Knights' War of 1522. Two years later, a far greater rebellion, the Peasants' War, spread through southern and southeastern Germany.

not just symbolic, for his career brought him into contact with two of the pivotal monarchs of his time: Augustus the Strong, elector of Saxony and king of Poland, and Frederick the Great, king of Prussia.

Augustus the Strong was justly named for his physique as well as his political power; immensely tall and muscular, he liked to fight bears and bulls in the public ring and to gallop through the streets of his capital, Dresden, holding the reins of his horse between his teeth and a street urchin in each hand. He personally designed the

palaces and pleasure gardens that made Dresden the most beautiful city in Germany; and he spent vast sums on art, ballets and pageants and on elaborate jewelry especially designed for his courtesans.

Most valuably, he supported research into the problem of producing Chinese porcelain, which, until then, had had to be imported from Asia at enormous expense. He was duly rewarded when Johann Friedrich Böttger, a ne'er-do-well chemist whom he kept prisoner in one of his castles, accidentally discovered the secret of making porcelain from local deposits of kaolin. The first European porcelain factory was established in a disused castle in Meissen, not far from Dresden, and Meissen (alias Dresden) china soon became one of the great luxury exports of Saxony.

After the death of Augustus in 1733, Berlin-born Frederick the Great emerged as the most popular ruler in eastern Germany. He had survived the rigors of his Prussian military education to become a philosopher-king, famous for his taste in art, music and literature. He wrote poetry himself and scholarly essays (in French, since he regarded the German language as fit only for peasants), played the flute, composed concertos and sonatas, and kept up a regular correspondence with Voltaire. Yet he also took an avid interest in military affairs.

As a young king, Frederick seized the rich province of Silesia from the Austrians. Then, in the Seven Years' War (1756-1763), he defeated the armies of Saxony and subsequently managed to hold his own on two fronts against the combined forces of Austria, France, Russia and Sweden. By the end of his reign, in 1786, Prussia had been trans-

formed into a major European power. For the next century and more, German history was to be increasingly focused on the city of Berlin and on the gradual ascendancy of Prussia over the other states of Germany.

This process was first impeded, then facilitated, by the French Revolution and the ensuing Napoleonic wars. Napoleon's armies had little difficulty conquering Prussia when — unlike such other German states as Bavaria, Baden and Württemberg — it refused to ally itself with France. Austria was also defeated, and it was Napoleon, in 1806, who finally dissolved the Holy Roman Empire — a venerable but then obsolete institution that Voltaire had sized up correctly as "neither holy, nor Roman, nor an empire." Henceforth the Hapsburg monarch was to be known simply as emperor of Austria. But in 1813, following the defeat of Napoleon's *grande armée* in Russia, Prussia joined the Anglo-Russian alliance, declared a "war of liberation," achieved a major

3

victory in the battle of Leipzig and contributed materially to Napoleon's final defeat at Waterloo. Thus, when the peace treaties were drawn up at the Congress of Vienna in 1815, Prussia gained vast new tracts of territory in both eastern and western Germany and emerged as potentially the strongest nation in central Europe.

In Vienna, representatives of the victorious anti-French powers had deliberated for a period of nine months on how best to redraw the map of Europe and ensure a lasting peace for the member countries. In respect to Germany, where the French Revolution had inspired popular demands for constitutional government and a unified state, the statesmen warily compromised by reducing the total number of sovereign states, at that time 200, to 39. These were to form the German Confederation, a loose union under Austrian presidency. The Confederation comprised the two giants, Prussia and Austria; the minor kingdoms of Bavaria,

Württemberg, Saxony and Hanover; various duchies and tiny principalities; and the free cities of Hamburg, Bremen, Lübeck and Frankfurt am Main.

German nationalism and liberalism now gained considerable momentum within the Confederation. Successive kings of Prussia, however, refused to liberalize their governments, and the Berlin regime, together with the Austrian government of Chancellor Metternich, acquired the reputation of being one of Europe's most repressive police states. Not until a wave of popular revolutions had swept across the continent in 1848 did Prussia concede to its people the rudiments of parliamentary representation.

In 1862, the gifted and iron-willed diplomat Otto von Bismarck became prime minister of Prussia. Two years later Prussian and Austrian troops jointly invaded Denmark and annexed the duchies of Schleswig and Holstein. But this conquest — which was followed by a dispute over the disposition of the

duchies — served to fuel the mounting rivalry between the two major German powers. In 1866, the Prussian army, with its murderous breech-loading needle guns, overwhelmed the Austrians in the Seven Weeks' War. This victory gave Bismarck a free hand to form a North German Federation of States north of the River Main, appointing himself federal chancellor, and so to take a giant step toward the creation of a united Germany that would be entirely independent of Austria.

In 1870, Bismarck maneuvered France into the Franco-Prussian War. It ended in January 1871, not only with the capitulation of Paris, but also with a carefully stage-managed meeting of German princes in the Hall of Mirrors at Versailles; there Wilhelm I, the reigning king of Prussia, was proclaimed *Deutscher Kaiser* of a new German empire — the Second Reich. This empire comprised 25 states, 12 duchies and principalities, five grand duchies, four kingdoms, three free cities and

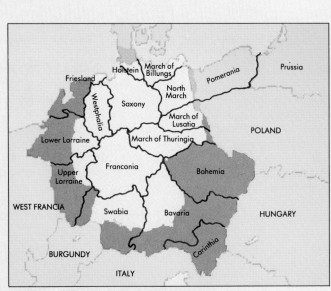

The German Empire in the 10th century.

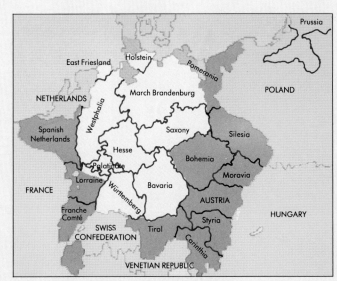

Germany after the Peace of Westphalia (1648).

vide diplomatic and military leverage against other powers. There was another reason for the Kaiser's naval buildup: Rapid industrialization and population growth had created an industrial proletariat, who lived under appalling conditions of poverty in the exploding urban centers in the Rhineland, in Saxony and the Neckar River valley. The policy behind colonial expansion, fostering dreams of imperial greatness and wealth, was designed to distract people's attention from these domestic problems.

Meanwhile the expressionist movement in German art and literature, born at the turn of the century, tried to provide a humanist alternative to the growing aggressiveness that pervaded the government of Wilhelm II. Such artists as Ernst Ludwig Kirchner, Max Pechstein and Max Beckmann looked beneath the impressionistic surface of things to discover the dark realities of life. Their dominant themes were anguish and compassion — for the urban poor, for victims of injustice, for mothers of dead children. "Truly it is not beauty and loveliness that are our strength," wrote the young sculptor and poet Ernst Barlach. "Our power lies rather in the opposite, in ugliness, in demonic passion."

The expressionist poets, feeling that the world was headed for disaster, tried to forestall it by appealing to the brotherhood of man. But these humane currents were weak by comparison with the mounting forces of militarism and expansionism: Europe had been transformed into an armed camp, and on June 28, 1914, the assassination of Austrian archduke Franz Ferdinand by a Serbian terrorist touched off the great powder keg.

On August 1, 1914, the German

A POSTAL PANTHEON OF MUSIC

The roll call of German composers includes a high proportion of the giants of Western music — a glorious heritage in which Germans have always taken pride. The postage stamps here — some issued by East Germany, some by the Federal Republic, others by prepartition governments — offer one small proof of the nation's esteem.

Spanning four centuries, the composers here not only expanded the musical horizons of their own times, but live on in the repertoire of artists performing worldwide. They comprise Telemann, prolific genius of the baroque era; Johann Sebastian Bach, master of sacred and secular composition; Handel, noted for soul-stirring

choral music and concertos; the monumental and tormented Beethoven; Weber, known as the father of musical romanticism; Schumann, author of brilliant piano and chamber works; Wagner, whose operatic cycle *The Ring of the Nibelungen* drew on heroes from the German past; Brahms, creator of symphonies, sonatas, and songs inspired by folk music; and Richard Strauss, composer of lavish operas and symphonic poems.

The nine are only a sampling from a great cultural tradition still very much alive today. Nurtured in its early days by the patronage of dukes and princes, German music east and west now benefits from opera houses, concert halls and state-subsidized schools.

3

government declared war on Russia; and within a period of just five days, Germany declared war on France, Britain declared war on Germany, and the Austro-Hungarian Empire declared war on Russia. The German army immediately marched into France and into neutral Belgium, confident of being able to repeat its swift victory of 1870. Instead, the army became bogged down in a bloody four-year war of attrition, in the east and in the west. All the major belligerents suffered enormous casualties on the front lines. Germany and its ally, Austria, were further hurt because of food and raw-material shortages caused by a naval blockade that the British organized.

Aroused most of all by Germany's unrestricted submarine warfare, the United States entered the war in 1917 and rushed fresh troops to France in time to thwart the last-ditch German offensive in the spring of 1918. With civilian morale almost at a breaking point and the Western front about to collapse, Wilhelm II was forced to abdicate and go into exile. On the same day, November 9, the Social Democrats—the only political party that still commanded mass support in Germany—proclaimed the establishment of a republic and began to go about organizing a provisional government. Then, on November 11, the armistice was signed. Firing ceased at 11 a.m., but in Germany another struggle, brief yet critical, was just beginning: the confrontation between those forces who supported a parliamentary republic and those who sought to establish a socialist or communist system.

The Social Democrats were fully prepared when left-wing riots broke out in December 1918 and January 1919. They had made a deal with the generals by which it was agreed that the imperial army would help to maintain law and order, and in return, the Social Democrat government would leave the army organization intact. Furthermore, it was arranged that volunteer units—financed by industry and constituted by army officers—should be formed to quell left-wing challenges to the government's authority. These units, called the Free Corps, attracted right-

On Christmas Day 1914, during a brief truce in the World War I battle zone, German troops in the trenches celebrate by decorating the traditional tree. Pictures like this, taken by official war photographers, were sent home from the front to boost public morale.

wing extremists who were to show excessive zeal in stamping out, rather than quelling, political opposition to the Social Democrats.

The first major clash of arms came early in January when an uprising was staged in Berlin by various left-wing factions, including the Spartacus League, a political group named after the leader of a slave revolt in ancient Rome and partly inspired by the Russian Revolution of 1917. This group, the forerunner of the Communist party of Germany, was demanding the creation of a democratic republic of workers' councils and also seeking to prevent the reemergence of the old capitalist-imperialist forces, which they held responsible for Germany's plight at the end of World War I.

The Spartacus League's attempted coup, badly led and ill-conceived, had no chance against the government troops. Many rebels were shot down in cold blood before the street fighting ended on January 12. Then, on January 15, members of the Free Corps hunted down, arrested and murdered the two most important leaders of the league, Karl Liebknecht and Rosa Luxemburg, thus creating revolutionary martyrs who are now exalted in the history books of East Germany.

Four days afterward, elections for a National Assembly were held. The assembly was convened at Weimar on February 6 to draft the constitution, and subsequently Friedrich Ebert, leader of the Social Democrats, was elected the first president of the new democratic republic. This was commonly known as the Weimar Republic, but Berlin remained the capital and cultural center, and there the law continued to be administered by veteran judges and civil servants who had never

Kämpfende Spartakisten.

fully accepted the new regime. Furthermore, German industry continued to concentrate wealth and power in the hands of a privileged few.

Thus the Weimar Republic began its 14-year life span with many handicaps; and it gained still greater ones on June 18, 1919. That day the Treaty of Versailles was signed in the Hall of Mirrors, where the German empire had been inaugurated in 1871. It caused Germany to lose about 13.5 percent of its prewar territory, including Alsace-Lorraine (which was ceded to France), northern Schleswig (ceded to Denmark), and West Prussia and almost all of Posen (ceded to Poland). In the process, Germany lost about 10 percent of its population. And later the Allies presented their crippling bill for war damages: 132 billion gold marks to be paid by

Germany in 59 annual installments.

These astronomical reparations contributed to a disastrous period of inflation. Before World War I, an American dollar was worth 4.20 marks. By mid-November 1923, shortly before the introduction of a stable currency, one dollar was worth 6,600 trillion marks. The climate was now ideal for the growth of extremist parties: The Communists gained marked support in Saxony and Thuringia, and they launched a short-lived uprising in Hamburg; and the following month, in Munich, a relatively new party — the National Socialists (Nazis), led by Austrian-born Adolf Hitler, an unemployed postcard painter and disgruntled war veteran — tried to coerce the right-wing Bavarian government into joining a revolutionary march on Berlin.

THE NAZIS' RISE TO POWER

In the fall of 1919, the Munich-based Nazi party — then known as the German Workers' party — was a palpable farce. It was without effective leadership, organization or policy; it had a membership of only a few dozen malcontents and its total assets were DM 7.50 (about $1.70). Just 14 years later, it was the sole political party of a nation of 66 million people.

The Nazis' meteoric rise to power was essentially the work of one man — Adolf Hitler. In 1919, he joined the party as an army corporal who had been twice wounded — and twice decorated for bravery — in World War I. He was also a fervent nationalist and gifted rabble-rouser and soon dominated his cohorts. In 1920, he renamed the group the National Socialist German Workers' party, or Nazis. Then he had the swastika and the "Heil" salute adopted as symbols.

He also recruited a private army of brown-shirted Storm Troopers, *die Sturmabteilung* (SA), to guard his meetings and intimidate opponents. But Hitler's most effective weapon was his oratory. Intuitively, he played on the fears of the Germans in the postwar climate of economic crisis and social unrest; unendingly he blamed Germany's misfortunes on foreigners, Jews, Communists and the weak German government, which had accepted the crippling terms of the Treaty of Versailles.

In 1923, Hitler made his first bid for power. Supported by some 600 armed followers, he seized Bavarian state leaders in a Munich beer hall, fired a shot into the ceiling and cried, "The national revolution has begun." But the following day, he led a mass march that clashed disastrously with the police. Sixteen Nazis and three policemen were killed; Hitler and nine others were arrested and tried for high treason.

Hitler, who was to serve only nine months of a five-year sentence, brilliantly exploited his trial to make himself one of the most talked-about figures in Germany. More importantly, the "Beer Hall Putsch" taught him patience and convinced him that the way to power was through ballots, not bullets. The Great Depression of the 1930s provided the climate for a dramatic Nazi revival. In 1928, the Nazi party had only 12 of the 608 seats in the Reichstag parliament. In 1932, with 230 seats, it was by far the largest political group in Germany. The following year, Hitler became chancellor and began to contrive — by legal means and by bloody intrigue — to establish an absolute dictatorship.

Bare-chested Nazis mock a ban on their uniforms.

Leaders of the 1923 *Putsch* meet at their trial.

A standard bears the swastika, the Nazi symbol.

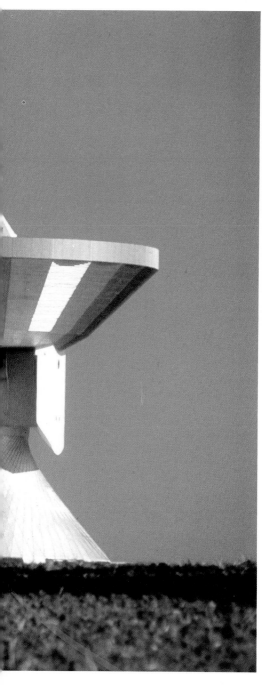

THE ECONOMICS OF SUCCESS

In July 1945, two months after Hitler's heirs had surrendered unconditionally to the Allied armies, U.S. military governor Lieutenant General Lucius D. Clay moved into his office in the American sector of Berlin and took stock of Germany's bitter postwar harvest. "The city was paralyzed," he later reported. "Shortage of fuel had stopped the wheels of industry. Suffering and shock were visible on every face. Police and fire protection had broken down. Almost 3,000 breaks in the water mains were still to be repaired. Ambulances were not available and transport of the sick and dead was by hand-stretcher or cart. Bodies remained in canals and lakes and were being dug out from under bomb debris."

This was *Stunde Null* — Zero Hour — as Germans dubbed the nadir of their fortunes at the end of World War II. Ninety-five percent of Berlin's center had been destroyed by bombing and street fighting, and in the rest of the rat-infested city only one house in four was still habitable. Most of Germany's other major cities had suffered on a comparable scale.

Altogether, more than three million homes were lost. The devastated areas were buried under an estimated 14 billion cubic feet of rubble, and from the ruins, there rose the stench of the entombed dead.

Not only houses had gone; a large section of Germany's industrial infrastructure had been obliterated. Many power plants, docks, railroad bridges, canals and telephone exchanges were in ruins. A total of nearly 250,000 tons of bombs, dropped on the transportation systems of the European battle zones between October 1944 and March 1945, had virtually cut Germany off from the outside world and halted communications within the country itself. Meanwhile, through this apocalyptic land traveled the dispossessed: bombed-out, evacuated families, expellees from Germany's former territories in the east, refugees from the Soviet zone of occupation, returning prisoners of war, and men and women who had worked as slave laborers under the Nazis. In the spring of 1945, two out of every five Germans were on the move. A year later, the number of expellees and refugees in the three Western zones exceeded five million; by 1950 it had risen to seven million.

Hunger drove this vagrant army — hunger and the search for shelter, fuel and clothing. On each day in August of 1945, 4,000 Berliners died of malnutrition, and half the babies born that month failed to survive. At the end of the year, it was found that only 12 percent of the children in Cologne had a weight normal for their age. While U.S. occupation forces were given a daily ration of 4,200 calories, Germans in some parts of the country were making do with a mere 700 calories per person per day — less than half the amount prescribed by the League of Nations in

Three churches that rose conspicuously above the wartime rubble of Frankfurt in 1945 *(below)* are now barely visible among new high-rise buildings housing banks and insurance companies *(right).* Frankfurt has been a major financial center since the 16th century.

1936 as the minimum necessary for an adult. In the British zone, the ration dropped in some instances to only 400 calories per day — less than the figure for inmates of the Bergen-Belsen concentration camp under the Nazis.

Since World War I, highly industrialized Germany had depended on exports of manufactured goods to pay for its food, but in the immediate aftermath of the war industrial production was at a halt. Eventually, with the rubble cleared away, it was found that most of the bomb-damaged factories were salvageable, but there was little incentive to get the wheels of industry turning again since it was impossible to obtain raw materials — not even the coal to fuel the fires of industry. The coal was there to be mined, but there were no textiles to clothe workers, no rubber for the air hoses of pneumatic drills, no watches to regulate shifts or alarm clocks to get the miners out of bed, no light bulbs to illuminate underground work, no transportation system to get the coal to the factories.

During the closing weeks of World War II, Hitler had told Albert Speer, Minister for Armaments and War Production, "If the war is to be lost, the nation will also perish. This fate is inevitable. There is no need to consider the basis even of a most primitive existence any longer." At Zero Hour — Germany's lowest ebb since the Thirty Years War ended in 1648 — it seemed the Führer had not exaggerated. To Germans and non-Germans alike, there seemed little hope that the defeated nation could climb out of the abyss into which it had plunged.

Anyone who witnessed Zero Hour and returned to Germany 20 years later could be forgiven for having imagined that they were in a different country. In place of the four Occupation zones there were two Germanys. In West Berlin, where Governor Clay had looked out at a city so choked with rubble that the postwar British Labor Government had estimated that it would take 30 years simply to remove the debris, the streets were lined with modern apartment complexes, offices, banks and factories. Throughout West Germany, more than five million dwellings had been built on the ruins of the old. The stores were crammed with washing machines, televisions, radios and other consumer goods; these were the same German makes that were being offered for sale in London, New York and Paris — indeed, in any country whose consumers could afford to pay for goods that were rapidly acquiring the reputa-

tion of being the best in the world. On the streets, Mercedes, Porsches and BMWs moved among the swarms of more common Volkswagens.

In the German Democratic Republic in 1965, the signs of affluence were much less marked. However, in the capital, East Berlin, only the occasional bomb site bore witness to the destitution of the immediate postwar years. In Alexanderplatz, the restored main square dominated by modern high-rise complexes, there was an exhibition that included bars of gray, coarse soap, pots made from steel helmets, sieves contrived from gas-mask filters, and old shoes patched with cardboard. Beside these relics from the postwar years, a sign asked: "Can you still remember?"

Four years after the building of the Berlin Wall and the stabilization of the

GDR work force, East Germany's economy had only just begun to make impressive progress. In West Germany, statistics confirmed — as living standards suggested — that a miraculous recovery had already been achieved. Between 1950 and 1964, the Federal Republic had increased its gross national product threefold, its gold and currency reserves by more than 2,000 percent, its exports by more than 500 percent. On the average, its industrial growth had been twice that of the United States. In 1964 it was second only to the U.S. as an exporter of goods and a producer of automobiles.

This totally unforeseen economic revival captured the imagination of the Western world. *Wirtschaftswunder,* "economic miracle," journalists called it, and indeed there seemed to be some-

thing providential about the amazing scale of the recovery. It was, of course, essentially dependent on the immense will and ability of the German people to work hard and conscientiously when the need arose. In the 1950s, West Germans had the longest working week in Europe (48 hours, on the average) and they were renowned for their efficiency. Such diligence, however, does not adequately explain this astonishing recovery. Numerous other factors, by chance and by design, converged to make it possible.

At Zero Hour Germany's economic potential was, despite the surface damage, surprisingly strong. Four years of intensive bombing had, in reality, destroyed only about 10 percent of the country's factories and plants — so little, for example, that on the eve of de-

feat the Ruhr was still producing more steel than at any time since 1939. For several years after the war, the shortage of coal and lack of transportation facilities held back industrial production. Dismantling for reparation also reduced Germany's industrial capacity. But in the British and American zones of occupation, at least, dismantling was limited, amounting to only 5 percent of industrial machinery. Moreover, in the long run it proved to be advantageous to some dismantled industries that they were compelled to reorganize completely with modern machinery and equipment.

One such industrial giant was the August Thyssen Hütte in Duisburg, prewar Germany's largest steel producer. Although it was attacked 96 times by Allied bombers in 1944 and 1945, it was largely intact at the end of the war. However, by the time dismantling was halted in 1949, it had lost 118,000 tons of machinery and equipment and 80 percent of its work force; production was down from more than 2 million tons to only a few hundred thousand tons a year. Nevertheless, under the leadership of Hans-Günther Sohl, the virtually dismembered industrial complex was soon rebuilt and it became the largest and most modern steelworks in Europe. And by 1973 it was the third-largest steel company in the world, behind Nippon Steel of Japan and the United States Steel Corporation.

None of this could have been achieved without massive investment, and though postwar Germany seemed superficially an investor's nightmare, the fact that Sohl received the necessary financial backing shows that the potential for economic growth was recognized. Economists sometimes estimate a country's investment potential by cal-

95

4

culating the relationship of industrial capital stock to the size of the available work force; if the amount of capital per head is low, the potential for productive investment is high. This was the case in West Germany in 1948: the increase of industrial machinery between 1939 and 1948 amounted to about 11 percent, but the growth of the available labor force far outstripped this figure.

Although Germany had lost more than 4.5 million citizens in the war, migrations of expellees and refugees actually produced an increase in population in the Western zones. By 1948 this amounted to a 20 percent rise over the population level of the same area in 1939. The potential labor force did not expand as rapidly as the general population; nevertheless, in 1948 there were almost 18 percent more people available for work than there had been in 1936. This labor force provided a huge

reservoir of highly skilled workers for all branches of industry; at the same time it created a gigantic consumer market and stimulated the construction of housing.

Different dates have been given for the beginning of West Germany's economic revival, but many experts judge that it was the currency reform of June 20, 1948, that launched the recovery. Under this reform, introduced by the Western Allies as a means of destroying the dominant black market and barter economy, the discredited Reichsmark was replaced in their zones by the Deutsche Mark (DM). Every citizen was at first limited to DM 40 in exchange for 40 old marks, and later another DM 20 was allotted on a one-for-one basis. Thereafter, funds held in Reichsmarks were redeemed at the rate of 15 to 1.

The reform was received by West Germans with mixed feelings. On the

one hand, it virtually eliminated at a stroke the entire debt of the former Reich. On the other hand, it reduced the value of the mark by 93 percent. The key point, however, was that the new Deutsche Mark actually had purchasing power — even if its value was based on the hopes and expectations of its recipients rather than on any supporting reserves of gold or silver. The new issue was so small that everyone was short of money. All at once, for the first time since the war, cash was in greater demand than material objects; and so storekeepers and tradesmen immediately put their hoarded goods on the market.

Soon afterward, the Munich newspaper *Süddeutsche Zeitung* described the reaction — and incidentally used the word "miracle" for perhaps the first time in connection with the West German economy. "The new German mark has wrought miracles. It has brought out the hoarded stocks and has filled many store windows. The new mark has stimulated overnight a great deal of growth. Now, all of a sudden, you can get folders, brushes, snaps, thermos bottles, shoelaces, buttons, tools, heat-resistant milk pans, frying pans for electric stoves, penknives, every sort of needle, rubber bands, floor wax, leather gloves, ties. . . ."

But it was not the currency reform alone that set the economy moving forward in June 1948. Equally important was a bold gamble by Ludwig Erhard, newly appointed director of the Economic Administration of the joint British and American zones. Two days after the currency reform, he announced the end of rationing and plans for the abolition of the intricate network of price and wage controls that had survived the fall of the Third Reich. His

In an East Berlin factory, a welder works on a component for a barge for use on East Germany's waterways. Following reforms in 1963, wages and bonuses in shipbuilding and other nationalized industries have been linked with profits in an effort to raise productivity and improve standards.

announcement was received with howls of protest from Germans who feared that the abolition of controls would cause prices to soar. Initially, prices did rise; in response, the trade union movement called a one-day general strike, and demonstrators marched with signs proclaiming "Erhard to the gallows." But Erhard refused to reverse his decision, arguing that the shortage of goods would stimulate the consumer-oriented industries and thus inevitably dampen inflation. He was eventually proved right. By the mid-1950s, prices of food, clothing and other necessities had begun to drop; and over the next decade the cost-of-living index rose only 16 percent, compared with 45 percent in Britain and more than 50 percent in France.

Ironically, this boost to the economy was administered by Allied officials who only three years earlier, in the bitter atmosphere of the war's aftermath, had agreed that the defeated nation should be kept economically crippled for generations to come. Now times had dramatically changed; the Western powers and the Soviet Union had taken up their polarized positions, and the United States especially was alert to the danger that Communism would gain credibility in an economically crippled West Germany. In December 1949, the newly founded Federal Republic began to receive American economic aid under the European Recovery Program, popularly known as the Marshall Plan after the man who proposed it, U.S. Secretary of State George Marshall. In the next five years, the Americans pumped more than 1.4 billion dollars of aid into the West German economy.

Necessarily, the farmers were among the first beneficiaries. Agricultural production rapidly advanced with in-

Under construction near Bremen, a coastal rescue ship receives a double aluminum shell to withstand rough seas and ice off Germany's north coast. The marine construction industry is concentrated in Hamburg and the Bremen area on the North Sea, and Kiel on the Baltic.

COLLECTIVE CRAFTS IN A SOCIALIST STATE

In the Erzgebirge mountains on the East German border with Czechoslovakia, south of Leipzig, a 300-year-old handicraft tradition flourishes as strongly as ever. Almost all the traditional wooden Christmas toys and decorations — animals, angels, nutcrackers — sold in East and West Germany are made in the village of Seiffen, where carved toys have been produced by local families without a break since the 17th century.

Even in the nationalized economy of East Germany, the toy-makers of Seiffen — some 60 percent of a population of about 4,000 — are self-employed, since state ownership has never been systematically undertaken in the sector of handicraft production. But, as with many of the East German cottage industries, most of the craftsmen are organized into either combines or collectives.

Each combine distributes annual dividends similar to the bonuses paid in the nationalized enterprises and helps its members invest in modern laborsaving equipment. The international market for these wooden toys is a vigorous one, especially at Christmas. Some 50 percent of the output is exported, providing a valuable source of foreign currency.

For a craftsman in a modern cooperative, an electric lathe makes the production of tiny carvings quicker than it was for his predecessors (*above, left*).

A troop of tiny painted animals is mustered in front of Noah's ark.

creased use of machinery and fertilizers; and this helped to hold down food prices at a time when incomes were low. But no injection of capital could rectify fundamental weaknesses in the structure and organization of German agriculture. Quite simply, there were far too many small, impractical farming units. More than half of all farms were incapable of supporting four or more families, an overwhelming majority were small holdings run entirely by a single family, and fewer than a third of all farms were economically viable. While productivity continued to rise throughout the 1950s and 1960s, the number of farms declined by one third and the agricultural work force fell from five million to 2.2 million. This followed a pattern of decline that began in the 19th century, when about three quarters of all of Germany's population was engaged in farming. The decline has continued: In the mid-1980s only 1.6 million people — less than 7 percent of the West German labor force — work in agriculture, stock raising, forestry and fishing.

Agriculture was the one sector of the economy that did not experience a postwar "miracle." In 1950, the Germans most shrewdly put the largest share of their Marshall Aid to the best long-term use by channeling the funds into industrial sectors that were short of the capital necessary for essential plant modernization. Industries that benefited most significantly were mining, steel, energy and transportation. Meanwhile, the economy was given another timely boost.

Unlike the conquering Allies, West Germany did not carry the economic burden of military expenditure in the immediate postwar years. On the other hand, the Federal Republic was in a po-

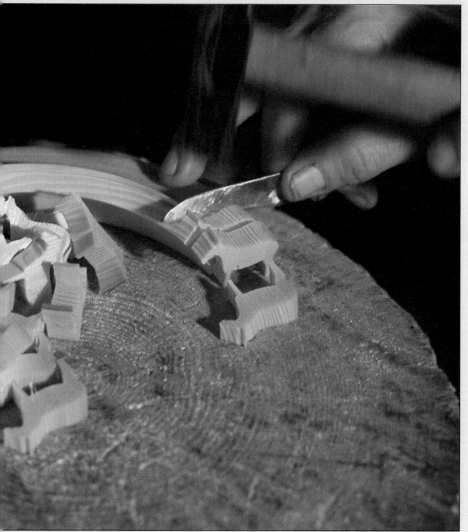

A ring shaped to a horse's silhouette on a lathe is cut into pieces that will be finished by hand.

sition to profit handsomely from the Korean War, which broke out in June 1950. During the months preceding the war, imports had been growing faster than exports; West Germany was seriously in debt to other members of the Organization for European Economic Cooperation (OEEC), the agency that handled Marshall Aid, and unemployment had risen to more than one million. Then the Far East conflict triggered a huge demand for iron, steel and heavy machinery — a demand that West Germany, with its great reservoir of cheap, skilled labor, was supremely well equipped to supply.

The "Korea boom" helped to solve West Germany's balance of payments crisis; and when the war ended in 1953, it was the Republic's trade surplus that was embarrassing, not its deficits. During this period, Britain's debts to West Germany steadily mounted; by 1954 they were so large that a British politician was heard to remark that the OEEC was "getting too tight for its clothes — one might almost say Professor Erhard was bursting out of them."

Professor Ludwig Erhard, son of a Bavarian tailor, was a corpulent man whose large cigar and expansive paunch had become the symbols of his country's growing prosperity. As economics minister from 1949 to 1963, he sought to develop a free "social market" economy — that is to say, an economic system in which the free play of market forces was tempered by a limited degree of government regulation to protect the weak, to hinder the growth of monopolies and to facilitate some redistribution of wealth. In practice, his form of economy was not greatly distinguished for its social consciousness, nor did it always adhere rigidly to market

principles. Nevertheless, his policies were undeniably a vital factor in the extraordinary progress of war-crippled West Germany — by 1964 the third economic power in the world.

Credit, too, must be given to Konrad Adenauer, the conservative leader of the Christian Democratic Union (CDU) and its Bavarian counterpart, the Christian Social Union (CSU). Adenauer became the Federal Republic's first chancellor at the age of 73 and served with undiminished energy for 14 years. He did not always agree with Erhard's economic policies. However, by way of statesmanship, he made a vital contribution to West Germany's economic growth. In November 1949, for example, his diplomatic skill persuaded the Western powers to cease dismantling in key sectors of German industry. Most notably, he was dedicated to the unification of Western Europe; and the climax of his efforts came in March 1957, when West Germany joined with France, Italy, Belgium, the Nether-

lands and Luxemburg in signing the Treaty of Rome to found the European Economic Community.

Meanwhile, under Erhard's guidance West German investment policy played an important part in assisting industrial growth. Tax concessions were granted to encourage entrepreneurs to reinvest their earnings, and industries that found it hard to raise capital were allowed to write off capital investments fairly quickly. Other government measures were to make overtime tax-free and to fix fairly low rates of tax on high incomes. By using tax concessions to pay for investment, Erhard effectively transferred resources from the general population to industry and the employers. At the cost of the consumer, industry had more capital to invest. At the same time, incentives were mounted to encourage industry to sell its goods abroad.

Government policy thus helped to set a pattern for the West German economy that has characterized its growth

In a Berlin plant of the Siemens company, West Germany's largest electronics manufacturer, a Turkish employee applies anticorrosive paint to a generator component. Germany's work force includes some two million foreigners, nearly half of them of Turkish origin.

INNOVATIONS IN TRANSPORT TECHNOLOGY

Designed for speeds up to 240 miles per hour, an electromagnetic train is tested at Emsland, near the Dutch border.

A highly sophisticated electronics and machinery industry has kept West Germany in the vanguard of transport technology. One current project is a revolutionary railway that eliminates physical contact between the train and the railway track. Thanks to the absence of friction, the hovertrain — which is drawn forward by magnetic forces — can travel safely and smoothly at speeds up to 240 miles per hour, double the speed of conventional trains.

Other West German innovations that are now being tested or are already in production range from a solar-powered car to a mobile airport terminal on wheels, from a computer-operated bus for 240 passengers to a small dashboard computer that can be linked into a highway control center to find the quickest way out of traffic jams.

ever since — namely, a combination of very high levels of investment, a strong export orientation and a relatively low level of the GNP (gross national product) going toward wages. Throughout the 1950s and 1960s, between 25 and 27 percent of West Germany's GNP went into capital investment, as against 18 percent in Britain. During the same period, wages amounted to only 47 percent of West Germany's GNP, as against 58 percent in Britain.

Apart from Erhard, the symbols of West Germany's economic success were the new millionaires — entrepreneurs and self-made tycoons such as Max Grundig, who built up an electronics empire from an eight-man company that assembled radio kits in a laundry in Fürth; Axel Springer, who started out with a guide to radio programs and came to own one of the largest publishing houses in the world; and Willy Schlieker, the shrewd wheeler-dealer who made his first million as a steel merchant, multiplied his fortune during the Korean War by anticipating the demand for coke to fuel the steel-producing furnaces of the Ruhr and then became a shipbuilding magnate.

Mavericks like Schlieker caught the public imagination, but they were not typical of the new breed of West German businessmen. A survey of the top German industrialists in the 1960s revealed that only 8 percent were owners of the firms in which they were working; the rest were managers. In the immediate postwar years, a new generation of men in their forties had moved into the important management seats. Like almost everyone else in the 1950s, they worked long hours and often neglected their private lives for the sake of their companies. Besides the Germans' well-known work ethic for exacting, hard work, their diligence may have stemmed, in part, from a sense that the taint of having cooperated with the Nazis had undermined the legitimacy of the professional middle

4

classes. And there was a strong tendency among managers to take on punishing daily routines in their almost fanatical pursuit of wealth and prestige. "Have you recovered?" was the question commonly put to managers returning from vacation.

But West German managers were not—and are not—mere drudges. A large measure of their success was due to their receptivity to new ideas from abroad. A survey conducted a few years ago found that a third of the top executives in industry had had working experience abroad, particularly in the United States. Moreover, West German executives tended to be more qualified than their counterparts in other European countries; three quarters of the top managers had a university degree or equivalent, while the figure for the younger men was nearer 90 percent.

Efficient managership, however, cannot ensure industrial success without the full cooperation of the workers, and therein lies another key aspect of the "economic miracle." During the critical first decade of reconstruction, German trade unions showed unusual restraint in the face of rising prices. Even when their country prospered, West German workers were rarely intransigent. For example, a particularly strike-torn period in Europe was from 1972 to 1973, but in the Federal Republic during this time strike action cost only 14 days per 1,000 employed persons, compared with 94 days in the Netherlands, 108 in Belgium, 231 in France, 700 in Britain and 1,449 in Italy. Furthermore, the regularity and scale of productivity increases in West German industry were due in no small part to trade union cooperation in the introduction of new technology.

In reality, though, West German

trade unions are not quite so docile as some of the statistics suggest. Their pay restraint in the early postwar years was, to some extent, the result of a chronic fear of inflation — something deeply ingrained in all German workers old enough to remember the catastrophic collapse of the mark in 1923. It can also be explained by the fact that their modest wage demands were balanced by strong bargaining for better working conditions and social benefits, which greatly improved the living standards of their members.

Later, the unions ignored the task of strengthening the factory organization and avoided work stoppages over local or material issues for a different reason: They were aiming for wider political power. Until 1952, the unions hoped that support for the Social Democratic Party (SDP) and the Christian Socialist wing of the CDU would enable them to achieve an ambitious program of establishing democratic controls over the economy and turning key industries over to public owner-

ship. When the unions realized that American influence and a consolidation of conservative forces in West Germany would deny them their goals, it was too late to turn to a policy of militant strike action. By then, the 1952 Works Constitution Law had been enacted. It circumscribed the powers of trade union officials, forbidding them to initiate strike actions and committing them to maintain company secrets.

At the same time, union power was enhanced by legislation that gave workers one third representation on the board of directors of all companies with 20 or more employees, plus a committee to protect employees' rights. This concept of social partnership was favored by the key groups within the trade union movement; indeed, it had general appeal in a country where so many people remembered that the Nazis had come to power by exploiting not only the differences between organized labor and employers, but also those within the three prewar trade union organizations.

Today, various factors discourage trade union extremism in West Germany. Closed shops are illegal. Political strikes are *verboten*. The unions are required by law to exhaust all other means of reaching a solution before calling a strike. A ballot of all members directly affected by an issue must show a three-quarters majority before strike action can be taken. And strikes are illegal during the lifetime of a collective contract. But these factors alone do not explain West Germany's impressively low strike record. In essence, that record is a reflection of German common sense and of traditional respect for order, authority and efficiency. "Why kill the cow you are milking?" was the question posed by trade union leaders in response to demands by militants during the seemingly endless years of economic growth and ever-greater benefits from the welfare state.

Meanwhile, the long-running boom presented employers with a novel problem: how to find enough workers to exploit the continuing potential for industrial expansion. In 1961, there were 500,000 job vacancies in West Germany and only 180,000 people unemployed. The economy was as vigorous as ever, and so the Federal Republic increased its efforts to recruit *Gastarbeiter* (guest workers) from abroad. Already it had job-recruiting agreements with Italy, Spain and Greece. Now it concluded an agreement that allowed the Federal Labor Office to set up job-recruiting offices in Turkey. At that time — the year when the Berlin Wall sealed off the main source of extra labor — no one could be expected to foresee that, 20 years later, West Germany would have 1.3 million unemployed and a foreign population of 4.6 million, including more than 1.5 million Turks.

It was not until the recession of 1966-1967 that West Germany's spectacular postwar growth came to an end. Three years earlier Erhard had succeeded Adenauer as chancellor. The recession — to some extent the result of overgenerous spending by his government — now proved that he had not, after all, found some magic formula for endless, trouble-free growth; indeed, Erhard's free market policy of limited government intervention finally had to be abandoned.

In 1966, the Erhard administration was succeeded by a grand coalition of the CDU/CSU and the SDP, which attempted to counter the recession by a greater degree of economic policy

Working around the clock on the assembly line of a BMW factory in Bavaria, robots weld the components of an automobile body. Automation plays an increasing part in West Germany's engineering industries: More than 15,000 robots were in operation in the 1980s.

MINERS' GUILDS: A RICH LODE OF TRADITION

A miner carries home his pick and lamp.

St. Barbara's image surmounts hammers.

Guild members support the miners' arms.

Every year on the 4th of December, the feast day of St. Barbara, patron saint of miners, West German coal miners don full-dress uniforms and plumed helmets and march to church in formal processions. They carry the picks and lamps symbolic of their trade *(above)* and display elaborately decorated banners *(left and right)*, treasured relics of the guilds that were formed in the mid-1800s to provide support for miners who were sick or injured and to fight for improved working conditions and better wages.

These local associations were the precursors of the single central trade union that today negotiates for the entire energy industry. But the original guilds live on as historic institutions with a loyal membership and a sense of tradition. Some 20,000 miners, working and retired, belong to more than 200 guilds representing the potash, iron ore and salt miners as well as workers in the coal fields of the Ruhr and other mining districts.

Clasped hands symbolize solidarity.

A banner shows Gneisenau's pit head.

A miner is framed by a wreath of leaves.

planning and by increased public expenditures, especially on the railroad network, road building and postal services. The new government was granted greater financial powers by parliament, economic forecasting was taken more seriously and regional aid programs were extended — most notably in the economically depressed Ruhr, where the entire coal-mining industry was reorganized with new capital to enable its survival in the oil age.

For several years, the West German economy flourished anew — even though the rate of inflation and the budget deficit increased. Then, in 1973, came a huge rise in oil prices, which was to be followed by another great increase in 1978-1979. West Germany, as a major importer of oil, was hit especially hard. The growing problems of industry were reflected in the falling rate of investment and in the increasing success of foreign competitors, particularly Japan, in the West German market. By 1982, the budget deficit had risen in one decade from a level equivalent to 18.2 percent of the GNP to 31.3 percent. That same year, when unemployment was approaching a record two million, the inability of the country's political leaders to agree on a strategy for economic growth precipitated the collapse of the 13-year-old coalition led by its long-serving chancellor, Helmut Schmidt.

These economic problems were not peculiar to the Federal Republic. All Western industrial countries were facing increasing competition from the Far East, and all had to cope with the effects of expensive energy. West Germany — despite the anxiety of so many of its citizens — had coped better than many others. Without significant oil reserves, the country would probably never again enjoy the same level of growth. On the other hand, with its highly advanced technology, its efficiently organized industry, and its wide experience of fighting inflation, the Federal Republic promised to retain a reasonably stable, if not always flourishing, economy.

During the 1960s it was not unusual to hear West Germans assert — sometimes with pride, sometimes in a patronizing way — that a second German miracle was being achieved: the "economic miracle" of the GDR. By 1970 that assertion was an indisputable fact. East Germany had become the 10th-strongest industrial nation in the world and, economically, the unchallenged leader of the Soviet bloc. Incredibly, the country was producing more than the whole of prewar Germany, which had had a population four times greater; and its production per head was almost one and a half times that of the Soviet Union. Czechoslovakian statisticians calculated that living standards in the GDR were more than 50 percent higher than in the Soviet Union; and every day, in East Berlin, Soviet soldiers could be seen ogling window displays of consumer goods unobtainable at home.

East Germany's economic recovery was not so swift or spectacular as West Germany's. Yet, in its way, it was no less a *Wirtschaftswunder*, because it was achieved in the face of greater odds. The German Democratic Republic was fundamentally handicapped from the start. First, its territory, the most industrialized part of prewar Germany, was not rich in its natural resources, except for huge deposits of brown coal (lignite) and mineral salts. In 1938, it mined only 1.9 percent of Germany's bituminous coal and only 6 percent of the nation's iron ore; and after 1945 it was cut off from its main sources of raw materials in western Germany. Moreover, while East Germany as a whole had suffered less war damage than West Germany, its loss in industrial capacity was infinitely greater as a result of Soviet reparations.

Soviet dismantling reduced the industrial capacity of East Germany by an estimated 45 percent, as opposed to the 8 percent lost in the Western zones of occupation. And the dismantling damaged the morale of the work force — especially when, as sometimes happened, plants were dismantled by the Soviets, laboriously rebuilt by the Germans, and then dismantled again. Dismantled plants were transported by railroad and sea and reassembled in the Soviet Union, where shortages of skilled labor often condemned them to stand idle for years. Recognizing the waste, the Soviets went over to appropriating the production of East German factories. Firms representing 30 percent of East German industrial capacity were taken over, including all major chemical plants, 80 percent of potash production and mining, and 40 percent of steelmaking. Between 1945 and 1953, the Soviet Union took an average 25 percent of the East German GNP without any compensation.

The Soviet hegemony also hindered reconstruction by forcing the GDR to rebuild its economy in line with Stalin's aim of completely eliminating dependence on imported goods. As a member of Comecon, the organization created by Stalin as a counterweight to the Organization for European Economic Cooperation, East Germany was obliged to develop an indigenous iron and steel industry at the expense of its more traditional and well-established

At the Krupps factory in Essen in the Ruhr, newly made locomotive wheels glow in the gloom as the steel cools. Munitions makers since the mid-1800s, Krupps now produces machinery for the chemicals industry and components for nuclear generators, as well as railroad equipment.

sources of income. Moreover, the members of Comecon were unsuitable trading partners for East Germany since most of them had underdeveloped, agriculture-based economies that could offer neither sizable markets for East German goods nor a differentiated range of articles for import into the GDR. And while the Western zones got free imports from the U.S. in the Marshall Aid program, the GDR had to contend with the unfavorable prices set for its imports and exports by the Soviet Union. In these circumstances, it was no wonder that more and more East Germans fled to the west, further weakening the economy.

How then was East Germany's strong growth rate achieved? Progress was possible when the Russians belatedly realized that the GDR, with its highly skilled, under-utilized work force and its long-established industrial base, was ideally qualified to be the "machine shop" of Eastern Europe. In 1953, the

Soviet Union returned to East Germany more than 200 industrial plants that it had taken over to supply reparations. Subsequently, expansion was especially marked in the chemical industry, heavy engineering and optical goods, and soon the member states of Comecon came to depend on the German Democratic Republic for chemical products, sophisticated machinery, tools and precision instruments.

But East Germany's economic recovery really dates from 1961. That year the building of the Berlin Wall ended the steady loss of skilled workers to the west. At the same time, the GDR was beginning to reap the harvest of its massive investment in education, with the emphasis on practical and technical subjects. A new generation of technically qualified cadres was emerging. The work force was further strengthened by an ever-increasing number of female workers. Some 70 percent of all East German women between the ages

of 16 and 60 went out to get jobs; by the 1980s, the number had increased, incredibly, to almost 90 percent: There were 4.1 million women out of a total work force of 8.3 million.

From the beginning, of course, state ownership was made the central element of the GDR economic system. The Soviet Military Administration had barely been set up in Germany when, in June 1945, the Red Army ordered the confiscation of bank assets and the closing of all banks. The next significant step was the expropriation without compensation of all land holdings of more than 250 acres, plus all holdings whose owners were judged to be Nazi activists or war criminals. More than 7.5 million acres were confiscated. One third of this land was administered by local authorities; the rest (some 5.25 million acres) was distributed to half a million farm laborers, industrial workers, and peasants and refugees from former German territories in the east.

The land reform, which had considerable popular appeal, instantly eliminated the *Junker* (landed aristocracy) as an élite group. The following year it was the turn of the industrialists to come under attack. On June 30, 1946, the people of the state of Saxony were called upon to decide in a plebiscite whether or not to nationalize "those firms and enterprises which profited from the war or are owned by Nazi criminals, active Nazis or war profiteers." There was a 77.7 percent vote in favor, and the Soviets decided that the result of this one *Land* reflected the opinion of all others throughout the Soviet zone. Consequently, some 10,000 businesses were nationalized; and, a few years later, many more private enterprises were squeezed out of business by a new, state-owned trading organization whose stores, often given priority in the delivery of supplies, came to dominate the retail market.

The last sector of the economy to undergo major reform was agriculture. Between 1952 and 1960, the farms of East Germany were collectivized and termed "agricultural production cooperatives." By the mid-1970s, about one tenth of all farms were directly owned by the state and the rest were state-controlled cooperatives. The only area in which private enterprise still played a sizable role was handicrafts, where private firms accounted for 60 percent of total output.

Such widespread public ownership has certain benefits. Because the profit motive is no longer the guiding principle for the investment of capital, the GDR is free from the cyclical fluctuations in investment and economic growth that have been experienced in West Germany. In agriculture, collective ownership enables East Germany

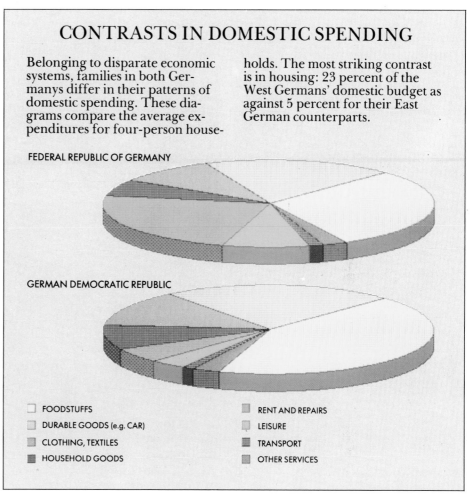

CONTRASTS IN DOMESTIC SPENDING

Belonging to disparate economic systems, families in both Germanys differ in their patterns of domestic spending. These diagrams compare the average expenditures for four-person households. The most striking contrast is in housing: 23 percent of the West Germans' domestic budget as against 5 percent for their East German counterparts.

FEDERAL REPUBLIC OF GERMANY

GERMAN DEMOCRATIC REPUBLIC

☐ FOODSTUFFS
☐ DURABLE GOODS (e.g. CAR)
☐ CLOTHING, TEXTILES
■ HOUSEHOLD GOODS

■ RENT AND REPAIRS
■ LEISURE
■ TRANSPORT
■ OTHER SERVICES

to reorganize land use and thus allows technical equipment to be used more cost-effectively than in the Federal Republic of Germany. Furthermore, in such an authoritarian state, trade unions enjoy much less independence, their primary role being to support the political and economic goals laid down by the party leadership. As a result, the economy has never suffered from organized strikes, although occasionally there are reports of brief, sponta-

neous protest strikes or slowdowns in isolated factories.

To be sure, all sovereign states in the Soviet bloc have these economic advantages. The important distinction in the GDR is that many of the problems of state and collective ownership have been avoided by greater flexibility and less dogmatism. For example, in transforming farms into collectives, the authorities were shrewd enough to allow farmers private ownership of sufficient livestock and arable land for their own personal needs. This cautious approach induced many of the farmers to give their grudging approval to the new system. Similarly, a lack of slavish demand for immediate public ownership characterized the crafts industry, where the continued existence of a large number of private handicraft enterprises partly compensated for neglect of consumer wishes in official economic policy.

In the 1950s and 1960s, the GDR leadership even made a major concession to private enterprise by encouraging the development of a number of seminationalized companies in which the entrepreneur and the state shared ownership, with the state providing capital. The most famous and successful of these was a textile firm run by Heinz Bormann, nicknamed "the Red Dior." Bormann's garments were worn by the wives of top GDR functionaries, including the wife of Walter Ulbricht, first secretary of the SED (1953-1971).

His clothing exports brought in so much foreign currency that he was able to silence party officials — who at one stage told him that his necklines were plunging beyond the bounds of East German decency — simply by threatening to quit the business. But in 1968, the Czechoslovakian uprising so unnerved East German leaders that they abandoned such bold experimentation with mixed ownership in industry. By 1972, all seminationalized firms, including Bormann's, had been

Soaring aluminum-clad columns support prism-shaped blocks of the Hypo-haus, headquarters of a Munich bank. Commissioned to create an alternative to modern office-building uniformity, the architects described it as "a caravelle with white sails billowing between silver masts."

taken over completely by the state.

The other main feature of the East German economy is central planning of production and exchange of goods; the production level of every firm, the places where its finished goods are to be sold, the prices to be charged for each product are fixed by a multitude of regional and industrial production plans that aim to fulfill the requirements of national two-, five- or seven-year plans for the economy. The advantage of such planning is that it allows the promulgation of clearly defined targets and priorities for the economy. This has been a major factor behind East Germany's industrial growth. Over long periods, 50 percent or more of the total investment in the GDR has gone into industry in conformity with national plans.

The disadvantage of central planning lies in its inability to cope with the complexity of economic life. This is particularly true of the GDR, which has the most advanced and complicated economy within the Communist bloc. By the time plans come into operation, the preparatory work has often taken so long that the statistical assumptions on which the plans rest are out of date. Moreover, the number of different authorities that are involved make the coordination of the various industrial, regional and individual plans extremely difficult, with the result that shortages and bottlenecks frequently occur.

An old East German joke runs: "Do the Swiss need a Naval Ministry?" "Of course. After all, we have a Ministry for Trade and Supply." Another tells of a customer who enters the Central Department Store on East Berlin's Alexanderplatz and makes his way to the underwear department, where he finds all the shelves bare. "Are you sold out

of underpants here?" he asks. "No," says the sales assistant. "I'm afraid you're at the wrong counter. They're sold out of underpants over there. Here we're sold out of vests."

Long lines and shortages are a very real aspect of everyday life in the GDR, but they are not to be viewed as a clear indication of an inferior German economy. In reality, the economies of the two Germanys have advanced at remarkably similar speeds since the 1960s. Of course, there are obvious signs of greater prosperity in the Federal Republic. West German workers, on the average, earn almost 40 percent more than their East German counterparts; some 80 percent of West German households have a car, as opposed to about 40 percent in the GDR; the average size of West German dwellings is much greater — 872 square feet compared with 538 square feet in the east. But such comparisons are in a sense misleading, since they fail to take into account the lower prices and taxation, and the greater equality of wealth in East Germany.

Quite simply, there are so many variables, east and west, that it is almost impossible to measure one German economy objectively against the other. Too much depends on the observer's point of view. What remains beyond dispute is that the average living standards in both geographical areas of Germany have more than doubled since prewar times. Remarkably, two sovereign states have achieved extraordinary progress while tackling similar problems with different socioeconomic principles. Only one factor is common to both success stories: the tremendous determination and energy of the German people in striving to climb out of the abyss of Zero Hour. □

The tallest structure in eastern Europe, East Berlin's 1,200-foot-high telecommunications tower dominates the main square, the Alexanderplatz. Visible from most of Berlin, the tower was built in 1965 as showpiece and symbol of East Germany's economic might.

A ZEST FOR LIFE'S PLEASURES

An old joke, originally told by easygoing southern Germans at the expense of dour, diligent Saxons, describes the events after a funeral. A young man, clutching an urn, says to his mother: "Shall I put grandfather's ashes on the mantelpiece?" "Certainly not," the mother replies. "Grandfather's ashes will go in the hourglass. We Saxons must always work, you know." The joke is at the same time prideful and self-mocking. Germans in general — not only Saxons — have long enjoyed an international reputation for being hard, efficient workers.

Now, though, the image is changing. The great majority have come to scorn the notion that work automatically takes precedence over the pursuit of personal pleasure. The shift in attitudes was spotlighted in 1982 by a major survey conducted by Hamburg's Leisure Research Institute. It found that work — in competition with family, leisure and friendship — came a shocking fourth in West German priorities; only eight years earlier, work had topped an identical poll. More shocking still, half of those under 30 claimed that they would prefer more leisure time to more money. It was as if the German people had decided that they had achieved a sufficiently high standard of living and that it was time to stop and enjoy some of the fruits of the *Wirtschaftswunder*.

Quite simply, Germany's steady rise in industrial productivity has brought not only an enormous increase in living standards but also a marked decrease in the labor needed to maintain those standards. Following the automation and computerization of industry, West Germans are enjoying a relatively short work week: an average of 36 hours — that is, two hours less than the British and four hours less than their Swiss neighbors. Moreover, West Germans have at least 10 national and religious holidays every year (as many as 14 in some predominantly Catholic *Länder*), and every worker has a legal claim to a minimum of three weeks' paid vacation. In fact, more than 90 percent of West German workers now have more than four weeks' vacation a year, and 50 percent of them claim more than five weeks.

Of course, West Germany's combination of affluence and leisure time scarcely came as a revelation to its European neighbors: For years this had been evident by virtue of German mass invasions of Mediterranean resort towns. As long ago as 1976, the Federal Republic overtook the United States — a country with a population four times as great — in its annual total of citizens traveling abroad. Since then the West Germans have become firmly established as the world's most inveterate tourists. Every year more than half of the population takes a vacation in a foreign country. Austria, Spain, Italy, France, Yugoslavia and Greece are the most popular destinations, and year

Dressed in medieval costume, a chubby-faced Bavarian turns a roasting pig on a spit at a historical pageant in the ancient city of Landshut. More than 500 folk festivals take place in Germany every year.

by year, an increasing number travel to far-flung corners of the world.

Moreover, after taking a three-week vacation abroad (three weeks is the length of time most favored for enjoying a complete change of environment and acquiring a well-finished suntan), West Germans usually have a week or two remaining for a second holiday, perhaps at home or in a neighboring country. There are many options from which to choose: a beach vacation on the North Sea, hiking in Bavaria, camping in the Black Forest, winter sports in the Alps or the West German half of the Harz Mountains. However, relatively few West Germans choose to take an extended vacation in East Germany. "It is not very good value for our marks," says a young business executive from Hamburg. "Anyway, we have so many other places to think about. It's strange: Towns like Zwickau and Cottbus, which were once a familiar part of every German's geography, are stranger to me than Nairobi and Katmandu."

In the GDR, the growth of leisure time has not been quite so dramatic. On the average, the East German worker has a 43.75-hour work week and 18 days' vacation every year. Longer vacations are usually granted to employees who have a greater length of service. People employed in a three-shift system — and mothers in full-time employment with two or more children under 16 — work only 40 hours a week. Those on shift work (some 40 percent of the industrial work force) get a minimum vacation of 20 workdays. There are also four national holidays and three religious holidays — two days for Christmas and one day for the Monday following Pentecost.

According to the holiday section of a GDR government handbook: "Travel broadens the mind; a change of climate is good for the constitution." In reality, only a tiny fraction of the population — excluding retirees — has an opportunity to take a vacation outside the Eastern bloc. Within the GDR, however, most workers are eligible for heavily subsidized vacations arranged by the travel service of the Confederation of Free German Trade Unions (FDGB). Under this system, families can spend a standard 13 days at a state-controlled re-

sort — usually on the Baltic coast, in the unspoiled southern highlands or the Harz Mountains — for approximately a third of the real cost. Similarly, other low-cost vacations are provided by more than 500 state-run campgrounds and some 250 youth hostels.

The main drawback for East German vacationers is not price but availability. The FDGB, for example, has 8.8 million members, but its facilities can cater to fewer than two million people every year. Even workers with sufficient seniority to be sure of an allotted place are rarely able to decide their own destination. Heinrich Müller, for example, is the foreman of a shift of 600 coal miners; with more than 25 years' service behind him, he is entitled to 36 days' vacation every year. He explains: "I have been to workers' hotels and vacation camps all over the country and on the Black Sea coast of Rumania. Every year we list our preferences, but the trade-union organizers decide where they'll send us. Everybody can't go to the beach at the same time. So we might apply for the Baltic and find we are going to Spreewald instead. But anyway,

Shaded by tall trees, a rustic holiday chalet (above, left) is a perquisite of a type enjoyed only by a small number of high-ranking East German officials. An ultramodern hotel (above), subsidized by the trade unions, is a more typical vacation accommodation for the majority of East German families.

wherever we go, we usually get excellent room and board."

Statistics show that in both Germanys there is a preference for beach vacations and group travel. East and West Germans have the same tendency to work hard at enjoying their vacations, quite reasonably regarding such leisure time as far too valuable to be squandered through lack of organization or planning. Even when Germans do not travel in a party, they are likely to form small groups soon after their arrival. Characteristically, too, many German vacationers are quick to stake out their own territory — perhaps going out before breakfast and leaving a towel to reserve a poolside chair or lay claim to a desirable patch of beach.

Until a few years ago, it was common practice — especially at the traditionally popular North Sea resorts — to mark territorial possession with a *Sandburg*, a huge sand castle that bears more resemblance to a field fortification than to a child's moat-and-turret creation. Essentially, this "castle" consists of a thick wall of sand, as much as three feet high, often decorated with seashells, and always large enough to encompass most, if not all, members of the family. In the years between the World Wars, it was not unusual for such ramparts to declare a family's affiliations by flying the black, red and gold flag of republicans or the black, white and red flag of monarchists. Alas, such energetic creativity has now been banned from

many beaches following complaints from weekend travelers who could not find space to stretch out in the sun, and — more influentially — from local traders who objected that *Sandburgen* were seriously reducing rentals of the *Strandkörbe,* traditional high-backed basket chairs big enough to shelter two people from the wind and to serve as dressing rooms.

Customs are changing so fast that it is no longer reasonable to generalize about the behavior patterns of German vacationers. For example, a new breed of West German tourist has been encountered at most European resorts: studiously unorganized young men and women, so casual in manner and dress that they make nonsense of the

113

5

old image of the German tourist as someone aggressive and assertive in the pursuit of pleasure. Nevertheless, the fact remains that this old image — or fear of the image — is still so strong that West German state governments periodically launch campaigns, urging politeness and circumspection upon those millions who have become the country's unofficial roving ambassadors. A few years ago, it took the form of a list of golden rules printed inside federal passports. The rules included the instructions: "Don't deny the fact that your parentage is German, but see to it that the foreigner is pleasantly surprised by it." And they concluded with the stern admonition: "If you are of the foolish opinion that everything outside Germany is worse, stay at home. If you think that outside Germany all things are better, don't come back."

In the Federal Republic the leisure explosion has by no means been limited to vacations abroad. At home, there has been a growth in leisure activity on a scale unimaginable even a generation ago. The boom began in the 1960s when billions of marks were spent by federal, state and local governments in a concerted effort to provide more and improved recreational amenities: playing fields, gyms, swimming pools and thousands of community centers with facilities for everything from ballroom dancing to basketball. Since then the number of sports clubs in the Federal Republic has risen to more than 50,000, with a total membership exceeding 15 million — or almost a quarter of the entire population. Association soccer clubs have the largest membership, followed by those for gymnastics, tennis, guns, track and field, handball, swimming, table tennis, riding and bowling.

This enormous membership is a reflection not only of the widespread availability of sports facilities but also of the German penchant for club activities. "When two Germans meet, they shake hands," runs an old saying. "But when three meet, they form a club." Indeed, about 40 percent of all West Germans belong to a club of some kind. For example, there are 14,500 choral clubs, with a total membership of more than 1.5 million; and there are clubs by the thousand for dog breeders, pigeon racers, stamp collectors, theater fans and, indeed, for aficionados of every conceivable hobby.

The club habit in Germany is a very old one. For example, the *Schützenverein* — gun clubs common all over the country — go back several centuries, and they still retain something of the air of medieval guilds with their ceremonial gatherings, their banners and badge-decorated uniforms. The majority are for men only, and membership in a gun club can convey considerable prestige within a community. There is no doubt that members spend more time lifting their beer glasses than their guns. However, each *Schützenverein* does hold an annual shooting competition to find out who is the best marksman. The prize is the decorated target used for the final rounds, and invariably the victor will mount it high on the outside wall of his house for all to see.

Equally prestigious are the *Freiwillige Feuerwehr*, local volunteer fire companies, formed in rural communities to deal with outbreaks of fire not large enough to necessitate calling professional fire fighters from the nearest large town. In its way, each one is a kind of club; its fire engine is provided by the state, but the members, all unpaid, buy their own uniforms, and as well as

taking part in regular training drills, they arrange various social events throughout the year, culminating in a grand parade. In some areas this is combined with the *Schützenverein* festival and inevitably ends with an alfresco feast and plenty of beer.

Drinking, in fact, is a major feature of club life in Germany. A whole subculture of clubs and semiclubs exists around the public barroom institution of the *Stammtisch*. A *Stammtisch* is, literally, "a table reserved for regular guests," but more generally the term is applied to any drinking fraternity that meets regularly. Such fraternities originated with the 19th-century trade guilds that used to meet to arrange deals and trade regulations; now they take various forms, ranging from informal political meetings to small groups of *Gasthaus* regulars sitting down at their own table to play a game of *Skat* — Germany's national card game for three hands, with rules so exquisitely complicated that they might have been designed to keep outsiders away. *Stammtische* are almost entirely for men, and about 20 percent of West Germany's adult male population belong to at least one. Exclusion does not seem to bother German women: A few years ago, a survey found that 43 percent of all *Stammtisch* "widows" were thankful to have their homes to themselves from time to time.

Clubs are an even more integral part of life in East Germany. Partly as a result of the state's distrust of anything resembling private enterprise, virtually every activity requires membership in an association, and those clubs that are not directly controlled by the Communist party itself will often come under the authority of a trade union. Such control does have some advantages —

most notably in sports. The GDR leadership regards success in international sports as an invaluable boost to East German morale at home and prestige abroad. Therefore it makes sports compulsory in schools, colleges and universities, and it spares neither time nor expense in developing young talent. By such single-mindedness the GDR has created a sports elite with a standing in international competition far beyond the reasonable expectation for a 17-million population. But success is bought at a price. Training is so concentrated that it displaces ordinary schooling, and those who fail to fulfill early athletic promise can find themselves handicapped in their pursuit of another occupation.

A massive increase in sports at all levels is one major aspect of leisure activity that East and West Germany have in common. Another is the sustained popularity of the performing arts: plays, opera, ballet, symphony. In the Federal Republic, more than 80 orchestras and concert halls are now subsidized by city or state. Of approximately 300 theaters, only about a fifth are privately owned; the rest, each with a permanent ensemble, are subsidized by the *Länder* or municipality and regarded as a community service. Per head of population, East Germany has even more theaters and concert halls, all owned and substantially financed by the state.

In both Germanys — as in all countries where television has mesmerized the masses — the small screen has partially eclipsed the large. Between 1956 and 1976, the period of most dramatic decline, the number of West German movie houses fell from 6,438 to 3,100 and yearly attendance from more than 820 million to a mere 115 million. Similarly, though less dramatically, GDR

A SUPER-EFFICIENT NURSERY OF SPORTS

A gymnast balances on parallel bars.

In the course of a few decades, the GDR has become a nation of athletic champions. The East Germans first made an impact on a global scale in the 1976 Olympics, when they won 40 gold medals, more than any other country except the U.S.S.R. Since then, they have become the most formidable contenders in the world of international athletics.

The GDR's phenomenal sports success is not the result of lavish expenditure on facilities and training. The state actually spends less on sports per person than West Germany. More significant is the single-minded determination with which it organizes sports activities and nurtures talent.

Since 1951, sports have been compulsory in all East German schools, colleges and universities. Any four-year-old in kindergarten participates in games or physical education every day. By the age of six, a budding gymnast or swimming champion will be encouraged to compete in local contests. Once in secondary school, most children take part in extracurricular games and classes, organized by volunteer coaches.

Underpinning the encouragement of sports through education is promotion by the powerful German Gymnastics and Sports Union (DTSB). Through branches and affiliations with trade-union societies and the 35 specialist associations for particular sports, the DTSB controls about 10,000 clubs and training facilities nationwide. It now has 3.5 million members — one fifth of the population.

The efficiency of the GDR sports machine, headed by a secretariat that supervises research and development, ensures that promising young athletes are guided expertly through the system. The most talented win a place in one of 20 special sports schools. These institutions usually take students at 13, though specialist education for gymnasts can begin as early as six.

The DTSB also runs specialist

clubs for other promising athletes. Membership is by recommendation only, and the clubs assume responsibility for training and also take an interest in the members' education and career prospects.

Critics of the East German sports system claim that state interest and attention is concentrated on the small minority who are likely to meet Olympic standards. But the German Democratic Republic is also committed to promoting sports activities for the masses. Approximately four million East Germans of all ages hold the GDR Sports Badge, an award for all-round physical fitness and skills whose motto is: "Ready for work and for the defense of our homeland." The right of every citizen to participate in sports and physical exercise is enshrined in the constitution and in the labor code. Upon leaving school, youngsters are encouraged to keep up their sports interests and general fitness in the workplace by entering competitions — such as the Most Athletic Girl Apprentice, with more than 400,000 entries in one year.

The state's dedication to the dual aim of individual excellence and mass participation in sports is expressed in a huge, two-part sports event held at Leipzig every two years: the Gymnastics and Sports Festival and the Spartakiad Games for Children and Youth. The festival includes contests and activities for all ages and levels of ability, and has more than 70,000 participants. But greater interest focuses on the Spartakiad, a testing ground for ambitious athletes, in which 12,000 youths between 13 and 18 years old compete. The winners are the elite of their age group — future Olympic contenders. But in the two years leading up to Leipzig, nine out of 10 young East Germans participate in local Spartakiads. Almost four million enter qualifying heats; more than a million reach the district finals; and about 100,000 go on to compete in county games.

Strength, grace and symmetry combine in a gymnastics display at the Leipzig Spartakiad Games.

Two guests stroll into the 330-foot-long arcade fronting the *Trinkhalle,* or pump room, a majestic building completed in 1842. A series of 14 frescoes by the 19th-century romantic artist Jakob Götzenburger adorn the walls, depicting local legends.

Inside the pump room, guests sip
large glasses of mineral water drawn
from the mineral springs. In late
summer and autumn, during the grape
harvest, they can opt instead for
the freshly pressed juice of grapes
from the region's vineyards.

As part of the thermal treatment in the Friedrichsbad, guests relax in the warm waters of a circular marble bath beneath the ornate central dome. Through the arch is another, elaborately decorated pool. Heron-patterned tiles *(right)* are typical of the gracefully detailed interior.

In the Augustabad, a client takes a therapeutic warm mud bath made with "fango," a local volcanic soil that is powdered and mixed with the thermal spring water. The Augustabad was built in the 1960s, but it boasts fittings of traditional elegance such as the brass-tapped sink on the right.

At Iffezheim racecourse, just outside Baden-Baden, visitors follow the runners of a race. Horse racing has been one of the principal attractions of the Baden-Baden season since it was introduced in 1858 by the Frenchman Edouard Benazet, son of the casino's founder, Jacques Benazet.

Guests in the private enclosure contribute to the high style of the August meeting, climax of the racing season. From kings and queens to opera stars, from sportsmen to industrialists, a glittering international elite has always frequented Iffezheim; in the 19th century, the French novelist Victor Hugo and the Russian writer Turgenev were enthusiastic patrons.

A couple crosses the stately drive of Brenner's, one of the most august of Baden-Baden's hotels. Established in 1873, Brenner's, with its own clinic, pool and treatment facilities, perfectly distills the atmosphere of unquestioned privilege and leisure on which Baden-Baden prides itself.

The staff of the renowned König's Confiserie and Coffeehouse line up behind a small selection of the shop's 98 kinds of cake and pastry. Since the beginning of the century, König's has served elaborate confections to its discriminating customers.

decided." Significantly, too, it is the young West Germans who have exerted the greatest pressure for keeping the concentration camps as memorials to the victims of Nazi persecution.

Herein lies one of the most striking aspects of Germany's development in the postwar years. In the free society of the Federal Republic, the reaction of younger Germans to so many anxieties has taken positive forms — repudiation of the old militaristic spirit that had grown so vigorously after Prussian-forged unification; rejection of old-style authoritarianism; demands for more democratic and Western-style institutions; mass demonstrations on behalf of nuclear disarmament and over a variety of environmental issues. In the process, West German society — its traditional values and behavior patterns — has changed dramatically.

Sociologists have argued that the emergence of postwar West Germans, more independent and progressive than previous generations, must be explained partly in terms of less disciplined family life. In turn, it may be argued that the seeds of this change were sown as long ago as 1919, when the Weimar constitution proclaimed equal rights for women. Subsequently, during the lifetime of the Weimar Republic, millions of women, many of them married, went out to work, so eroding the old concept of a male-dominated society where the German *Hausfrau* was consigned to the realms of *Kinder, Küche und Kirche* (children, kitchen and church).

This trend was briefly reversed by the Great Depression, then by the coming to power of the Nazis who provided financial incentives for women to become housewives and mothers. But later, as Germany prepared again for war, more than 14 million women were needed in full-time employment, and millions of children became known as *Schlüsselkinder* (latchkey children) because they returned to an empty house when school finished in the afternoon.

After the war, the number of women employees increased further. First, there were countless war widows who had to find jobs; and later, in West Germany, a booming economy encouraged wives to join the work force in pursuit of the material benefits of a rich consumer society. Between 1950 and 1969 the number of women employees in West Germany more than doubled, from 4.2 to 9.6 million. By the mid-1980s, well over one third of the total work force (10.2 out of 26.8 million) were women, and 3.5 million had children under the age of 18. So there emerged a new generation of Germans who experienced less parental control than before and who were exposed more and more to outside influences via the new medium of television.

Furthermore, as the Federal Republic became more closely integrated with Western democracies, discipline in the schools became less rigid. Before the division of Germany, east and west, the atmosphere in most classrooms had not

world as we know it. Disturbed by the proliferation of U.S. and Soviet missiles in Europe, some 450,000 West Germans joined this demonstration.

6

changed greatly from that experienced in the 1870s by the eminent dramatist Gerhardt Hauptmann, who later recalled, "When the teacher entered the classroom, the boys immediately stood to attention until the order 'Sit down' was given in a military voice. The way of teaching was exactly like that of an instructor in the army. Simple words, a mild manner, a kind support of the pupil were considered sentimental. They were regarded as weak and effeminate. Behind the teacher was not Lessing, Herder, Goethe or Socrates, but the Prussian sergeant." By the late 1960s, however, British and French children going to West Germany in school exchange programs were often surprised to find the atmosphere in classrooms relaxed and informal. In high schools, it was not unusual to encounter young teachers who wore blue jeans, and — much to the horror of older Germans — were on first-name terms with their pupils. Some universities were still bastions of privilege and outdated formalities. But otherwise the education system had received sweeping reforms.

Meanwhile, the advent of the *Pille* had heralded the beginning of a new permissive age. In the 1960s, Oswalt Kille's explicit sex-instruction books and films became all the rage; and bestsellers like his *Deine Frau, das unbekannte Wesen* (Your Wife, the Unknown Human Being) raised questions about the conduct of marital relations that many couples had never faced before. Inevitably, women's greater economic and sexual freedom had a profound impact on family life in West Germany, as indeed it had on the Western world in general. It led to the erosion of authoritarian conventions in the home and the emergence of a postwar generation prepared to challenge traditional values and authoritarianism in the world.

From the mid-1960s onward, a large segment of West German students were in a reformist mood, eager — after the democratization of the sociopolitical system — to complete what the eminent Bonn historian Karl Dietrich Bracher called emancipation from yesterday. They pressed for modernization of their social, educational and legal institutions. More ambitiously, they challenged the authority of the university professorate, or rather the authority of the senior, long-serving full professors, a prestigious group of mandarins whose exalted, tenured, highly paid and autocratic positions represented a supreme example of conservatism and elitism.

At first, the German student revolt impressed many foreign observers as an object lesson in grass-roots democracy. Tragically, however, the revolt became progressively more militant after a student, Benno Ohnesorg, was shot and killed by riot police on June 2, 1967, during a rowdy demonstration in West Berlin against the visiting shah of Iran. Thereafter, extremists began to take over the student movement and the violence escalated. Students forcibly invaded faculty meetings to present their demands for reforms, "to sweep away the mold of a thousand years." University buildings were daubed with political slogans. Professors were terrorized in their homes.

The German people had always held university professors in the highest esteem, ranking them above all other career groups, including bishops, generals and ministers of state. Disrespectful action on the part of student extremists now horrified older Germans, many of whom saw it as final proof that society had gone too far in its abandonment of traditional values and disciplines; public opinion hardened against the students. There were to be another six years of conflict before the university administration was radically reformed and students were given a share in the decision-making process.

More alarmingly, the killing of Ohnesorg had aroused young radicals whose motivation was ideological. A newborn June 2 Movement announced its intention of avenging Ohnesorg's death. And among those who broke with conventional, nonviolent protest was Gudrun Ensslin, a leader of the Socialist Students' Union, who turned to terrorism as the "logical" next step in her struggle against the government. She and a group of like-minded revolutionaries resolved to fight "police-murderers" with acts of violence: In their eyes, the government belonged to "the generation of Auschwitz — you cannot argue with them."

Eventually, this terrorist group became known as the Baader-Meinhof gang, so named after its protagonists: Andreas Baader, son of a university professor, and Ulrike Meinhof, a highly intelligent journalist and a mother of two children. In 1972, following a notorious career planting bombs and robbing banks, Ensslin, Baader and Meinhof were arrested; they were later sentenced to life imprisonment after facing charges of complicity in five murders and 71 cases of attempted murder. But this did not stop terrorism; instead the Baader-Meinhof gang spawned another, more lethal and professional, gang of terrorists, the Red Army Faction (RAF), which openly called for a socialist revolution. In April 1977, after Meinhof had committed suicide, these terrorists took vengeance by murdering the chief federal prosecutor, Siegfried Buback. Two months later, the gang murdered Jürgen Ponto, the chairman of the board of the Dresdener Bank, in a bungled kidnapping attempt.

Then, in the fall, there unfolded the most spectacular drama in the tragic history of postwar German terrorism. The remnants of the RAF kidnapped the president of the German employers' association, Hans-Martin Schleyer, killing his driver and three bodyguards in the process. They offered to exchange Schleyer for the surviving Baader-Meinhof gang leaders. Chancellor Schmidt refused to capitulate to their demands. Subsequently, members of the gang hijacked a Lufthansa plane on a flight from Majorca to Hamburg and forced it to fly on to Rome, Cyprus, Dubai and Aden before coming to a halt in Mogadishu, Somalia. En route, one of the pilots was killed

in cold blood and many of the 82 passengers were brutally maltreated by grenade-toting terrorists.

In Mogadishu, the kidnappers threatened to kill everyone aboard if their demands were not met. But before they could act, the plane was seized by a crack team of West German counter-terrorists, which rushed the plane in the middle of the night, killed three of the hijackers, wounded the fourth and saved all the hostages. Shortly afterward it was discovered that Ensslin and two other Baader-Meinhof terrorists had committed suicide in prison. The kidnappers retaliated by murdering Schleyer and leaving him in the trunk of a car found abandoned in Alsace, France, not far from the West German border. "The battle has just begun," they declared.

The Mogadishu incident marked a turning point in German radical poli-

tics. The terrorists' mindless cruelty had sickened and alienated all but the most fanatical of their supporters — who originally were thought to have numbered about 100,000 people, mainly students. It was not the end of terrorism. Since the early 1980s, the RAF has attacked NATO installations in Europe, focusing particularly on U.S. military personnel and property, and attempted to assassinate General Frederick Kroesen, commander of the U.S. Army in Europe. Then, in 1985, perhaps to strengthen their numbers, the RAF joined forces with the French terrorist group Direct Action, continuing to make NATO its main target. The youth movements, however, have become noticeably less concerned with ideologies since the Mogadishu drama, getting involved instead in environmental issues and alternative lifestyles.

How deeply West German youth had

Avant-garde artist Joseph Beuys *(above)*, **a supporter of West Germany's Green party stands among 7,000 basalt blocks that form part of a sculpture for the town of Kassel. The stones** *(left)* **are to be embedded in the earth, next to trees, to symbolize the power of nature. Beuys died in early 1986.**

A teacher monitors students' progress in the language laboratory at Leipzig's 700-year old Thomaner music school. J. S. Bach wrote much of his choral music for the Thomaner, one of some 100 schools in East Germany providing a general education and training for musically gifted children.

become concerned with environmental threats was reflected in 1981 by a poll of 15- to 20-year-olds, which found that 30 percent of the age group fully expected technology and chemistry to destroy the globe, while another 46 percent thought that such destruction was probable. At this time, more and more young Germans were questioning old values and attitudes. For example, when government officials argued that the expansion of nuclear research and development was essential for West Germany's highly industrialized economy, young radicals countered that such a purely financial argument — putting materialism before quality of life — was typical of the generation that had forged the *Wirtschaftswunder*.

For a while it seemed Germany was fated to stage a replay of the oldest Teutonic saga of confrontation between generations: the ninth-century tale of the veteran Hildebrand, who returned home weary from war, only to

be challenged to combat by his impetuous, uncompromising son Hadubrand. In the early 1980s, a recurrent image on West German television screens was the street battle: on the one side the experienced, plastic-visored, shield-bearing riot police, drawn up in a straight line like the knights in Eisenstein's film classic *Alexander Nevsky;* on the other, a motley crew of young protestors demonstrating for squatters' rights, for the preservation of some woodland threatened by an *Autobahn* development, for the cancellation of plans to build an atomic reactor or another office complex in an area that had a serious shortage of housing.

At the same time, ever-increasing numbers of West Germans (eventually more than 60,000 a year) were applying to be registered as conscientious objectors, and so take the alternative-service option to work in hospitals, nursing homes and institutions for the handicapped instead of 15 months of military

service. "Our young people are not nationalistic," said the chief of the Alternative Service Department in 1983. "They hardly know what the words 'German' and 'Fatherland' mean."

To a degree, West Germany was paying the price of the baby boom of the prosperous, optimistic 1960s — productive years that now released an unusually large number of youngsters leaving school for the job market at a time when unemployment was rising. In part, this explained the enormous increase in the number of young Germans practicing different lifestyles, the so-called *Alternativen.* By the early 1980s, there were hundreds of communes whose members were attempting to define, as one put it, "a culture alongside the traditional confining German society."

The mecca of this vast counterculture movement was West Berlin, where at least 50,000 residents had dropped out of the main stream of society. They included radical activists, squatters, members of health-food communes, sexual liberationists and religious visionaries. "Anybody who wants to be different and to feel all right being different, who doesn't want the things he or she was taught to want, flees to West Berlin," explained a writer for the alternative newspaper, *die tageszeitung.* Citizens of this free-thinking society established not only their own newspapers and magazines, but also their own food stores, restaurants, theaters, communal gardens, social centers. For some, drugs were an essential part of life; others were advocates of clean living who shunned all forms of drugs, including tobacco and alcohol. But the majority had one sentiment in common: contempt for the materialistic values of the consumer society.

free and compulsory system of education. As in the Federal Republic, school starts at about 8 a.m. and ends around 1 p.m. But then comes a very significant difference in the daily routine. While most West German children return home for lunch and tackle their homework (probably unsupervised if both parents are working), East German students — rarely left to their own devices — stay on for lunch and then for supervised Pioneer activities. Members may belong to various career-study groups, as well as orchestral, choral, theatrical and sports groups; and during school holidays they may attend Pioneer camps and join in organized visits to factories, military units, cultural and sports events.

In the early years at a GDR school, the timetable is dominated by German and mathematics, with sports, music, drawing and gardening as subsidiary subjects. At the age of 12, children have history, geography, biology and physics added to their curriculum, plus six hours of Russian every week. Their history textbooks differ significantly from West German ones. In the GDR, German history is strongly in favor of groups and individuals judged to have aided progress toward the creation of a "workers' and peasants' state." From the 19th century onward there is overwhelming emphasis on Karl Marx and his followers, from the martyred Rosa Luxemburg and Karl Liebknecht to the leading figures of the present-day Socialist Unity party.

East German and West German history books are equally condemnatory of Hitler's Third Reich. But here, again, there is a significant difference: GDR citizens grow up with a much more comfortable perspective of the Nazi era. They learn that the Nazis were essentially products of "monopoly capitalism," and unlike West German children, they are given positive heroes of the 1930s and 1940s to admire: Thälmann and the many other German Communists who died in concentration camps, plus a few "enlightened" non-Communists such as Count Claus Schenk von Stauffenberg, whose bomb nearly killed Hitler in July 1944. Thus, East Germans are freed of any sense of guilt. While the Federal Republic has paid out trillions of marks in restitution for the wrongs done to Jews, the GDR has paid none on the grounds that it is not the successor to the Third Reich and has no moral or legal obligation for the evils of the Nazis.

As though conscious of the danger of teen-age rebellion, the state makes a renewed effort to influence people from the age of 14. At that age, virtually all East Germans attend preparatory classes for the *Jugendweihe* (youth consecration) — an initiation ceremony, designed to replace religious confirmation, at which young people affirm publicly that they have "grown up in the Socialist faith." At 14 years, also, East Germans are eligible for the senior wing of the *Freie Deutsche Jugend* (FDJ), the Free German Youth movement, founded in 1946 with Erich Honecker (named head of state in 1971) as its first chairman.

The FDJ, with a membership of some 2.3 million (about 77 percent of all East Germans aged 14 to 25), wields considerable power and influence. It is represented in schools and factories, villages and urban residential areas, and has 40 representatives in the 500-deputy People's Chamber, the GDR's parliament. Its distinctive uniform — blue cap, shirt and trousers, and loosely tied red scarf — is prominent at political rallies.

It is also to be seen among the youth brigades employed during college vacations on collective construction projects such as building dams or extending railroads — a form of cheap labor that has made a significant contribution to the national economy.

On a less solemn note, FDJ members operate thousands of youth clubs, organize popular Rock-for-Peace pop concerts, and compete in *Spartakiaden*, multisport games held biennially at local, district and national levels. In addition, officials of the movement help to administer *Wehrerziehung* (defense education). Since 1978, this subject — mainly involving marksmanship, field training and first aid — has been compulsory for all boys of 15 and 16, preparing them for the 18-month military service that is mandatory for all male citizens between 18 and 26.

Thus, the FDJ effectively channels youthful energies into activities favored by the state. Inevitably, there comes a time when young East Germans are liable to rebel against so much regimentation and seek to express themselves in a more individual style. Indeed, some continue to adopt the outward fashions of the West's alternative lifestyle; the GDR has long-haired hippies, skinheads, leather-clad motorbikers, even bemohawked punks. But in this rigidly ordered socialist state, it is impractical to drop out of society. After all, there is officially no unemployment, and so there is no such thing as welfare or unemployment insurance. Here, a youth would need exceedingly generous parents or friends to survive without a job.

The difficulties that may be encountered by the nonconformist are illustrated by the case of Rudolf Schwartz, an assembly-line solderer in a Karl

In East Berlin's Pioneer Palace, with its free sports and leisure facilities, a girl spins on a wheel that simulates the weightlessness of space flight. Young East Germans' interest was boosted by GDR citizen Sigmund Jähn's flight on a Soviet space mission in 1978.

6

Marx-Stadt electronics factory. As a brilliant school sprinter, Rudolf automatically went to the State Institute for Physical Education, a university-level technical college in Leipzig. The college's main function is to produce professional athletics instructors, who are expected to maintain the GDR's phenomenal record in international sports. But Rudolf did not want to join the mainstream of the state's sports program. His ambition was to teach handicapped children remedial exercises.

He recalls: "All the emphasis was on producing winners. Everybody was taught that we had to win — win for the cause, win for the republic." Eventually he and several other students criticized the institute's official policy, largely on the grounds that "sports should be designed for people, not people for sports." There were arguments in class; later, confrontation with institute officials. The result: Rudolf, then 22, was summarily dismissed and blacklisted for life from physical education. Now he has a factory job that enables him to meet his basic needs but keeps him discontented. He hopes to find work in a small crafts industry that has not been nationalized — handcrafting leather bags or cutting designs on tombstones is potentially more lucrative than his present job. If he succeeds, he will have realized his other ambition — to maintain a low profile or, as he puts it, "to stay out of sight and not be answerable to any authority."

Günther Gaus, who retired in 1981 as chief of the West German mission in East Berlin, explained that in the GDR — which he found "more German than the Federal Republic" — they have coined the word, *Nischengesellschaft*, roughly meaning a society in which individuals carve for themselves niches where they can live beyond the far-reaching shadow of the state. In reality, though, only a very small minority achieve such freedom from authority. Here lives on the ubiquitous Prussian *Beamte*, the same stern-faced unbending bureaucrat who constituted the backbone of Imperial, Weimar and Nazi Germany. Now this bureaucratic type runs not only the city hall, the post offices, the railroads and the prisons, but the stores and factories as well. Here, too, authority is massively represented by the military: a National People's Army of at least 115,000 troops and 50,000 border guards. With the addition of an estimated Soviet force of 380,000 or more troops, East Germany is one of the most militarized countries in the world.

In this authoritarian state, the government's image of the perfect citizen is summed up in the old slogan that is still painted on highway bridges, *Aufmerksam, Rücksichtsvoll, Diszipliniert — Ich Bin Dabei!* (Attentive, considerate, disciplined — I am with it!). Actually, in spite of the relentless government propaganda, most East Germans are not wholeheartedly with it. They may be true socialists in spirit (long before the creation of the GDR, eastern Germany was the traditional stronghold of German socialism), but they resent the earnest, humorless functionaries of the *Apparat* who run the country and constitute the privileged elite.

The majority make obeisance to the Soviet-designed system because they realistically recognize that they have no alternative. As a Dresden factory worker reasoned: "Why waste time worrying about how to change something that cannot be changed? We had our little rebellion in 1953 and no one supported us. Since then our living standards have steadily improved. Not as much as in West Germany, of course. But at least no one is starving or homeless. So why risk rocking the boat? We prefer to keep quiet and have a reasonably comfortable life without all the protests and political fighting that so often disrupts life in the West."

Recognizing the ominipotence of the state, GDR citizens tend to concern themselves with problems of everyday life and — unlike the West Germans — do not suffer too much anxiety over large issues beyond their control or sphere of influence. The exception, of course, is dread over the proliferation of nuclear weapons in Europe. Because of the catastrophe of 1945, East Germans, as well as West Germans, have a deeply ingrained horror of war; and that horror is made all the greater by the realization that war in Europe would almost certainly commit the German people to fratricide.

It is the unique tragedy of the Germans that they seem destined to belong inescapably to twin buffer states. Reunification may remain a task set by the Federal Republic's Basic Law. West German chancellors may consistently proclaim that there is only one German nation. Nevertheless, the fact remains that foreign political leaders on either side of the great divide regard the existence of two Germanys as essential for the maintenance of the balance of power between East and West. The alternative — too alarming for neighboring countries to contemplate — is the re-emergence of a single nation-state of 78 million Germans, an industrial, commercial and military colossus that would dominate central Europe. Thus, as throughout the greater part of German history, national unity remains a seemingly impossible dream. □

Responding to the pulsing rhythms of the Rolling Stones, some 100,000 young West Germans enjoy themselves at an open-air rock concert in Munich's Olympic Stadium. In front of the stage, a fire hose plays over the heads of the crowd, providing welcome relief from the summer heat.

ACKNOWLEDGMENTS

The index for this book was prepared by Vicki Robinson. For their help with this volume, the editors also wish to thank the following: Bäder-und Kurverwaltung, Baden-Baden, Federal Republic of Germany; Bildarchiv Preussischer Kulturbesitz, West Berlin; Mike Brown, London; Deutscher Bäderverband e. V., Bonn; Embassy of the German Democratic Republic, London; German Historical Institute, London; Goethe Institute, London; Liz Hodgson, London; Jay Hornsby, London; Margit Hosseini, Embassy of the Federal Republic of Germany, London; Eluned James, London; L. E. Kramer, London; Landesfremdenverkehrsverband Bayern e. V., Munich; Jeremy Lawrence, London; G. Schäfer, Embassy of the Federal Republic of Germany, London; R. Tegtmeier, Embassy of the Federal Republic of Germany, London; Deborah Thompson, London.

PICTURE CREDITS

Credits from left to right are separated by semicolons, from top to bottom by dashes.

Cover: Ernst Haas, Magnum Distribution. Front endpaper: Map by Roger Stewart, London. Back endpaper: Digitized image by Creative Data, London.

1, 2: © Flag Research Center, Winchester, Massachusetts. 6, 7: Hans Wiesenhofer, Pöllau, Austria, digitized image by Creative Data, London. 8, 9: Cotton Coulson from Woodfin Camp Inc., Washington, D.C. 10, 11: Hans Wiesenhofer, Pöllau, Austria. 12, 13: Thomas Höpker from Agentur Anne Hamann, Munich, digitized image by Creative Data, London. 14, 15: Hans Wiesenhofer, Pöllau, Austria, digitized image by Creative Data, London. 16: Jürgen Schadeberg, Le Cannet, France. 17: Hans Wiesenhofer, Pöllau, Austria. 18: Digitized image by Creative Data, London. 19: Wilfried Bauer from Agentur Anne Hamann, Munich. 21: Cotton Coulson from Woodfin Camp Inc., Washington, D.C. 22, 23: Wilfried Bauer from Agentur Anne Hamann, Munich. 24, 25: Thomas Höpker from Agentur Anne Hamann, Munich. 26, 27: Friedrich Stark, Dortmund. 28, 29: Digitized image by Creative Data, London. 30: Cotton Coulson from Woodfin Camp Inc., Washington, D.C. 31: Thomas Höpker from Agentur Anne Hamann, Munich. 32-39: Frieder Blickle, Hamburg. (33: Digitized image by Creative Data, London.) 40, 41: Guido Mangold from Agentur Anne Hamann, Munich. 42: Bildarchiv Jürgens, Cologne; Thomas Höpker from Agentur Anne Hamann, Munich; Cotton Coulson from Woodfin Camp Inc., Washington, D.C. 43: David Simson, Bisley, England; Hans Wiesenhofer, Pöllau, Austria (2). 44: Hans Wiesenhofer, Pöllau, Austria. 45: Dirk Reinartz from VISUM, Hamburg. 46: Digitized image by Creative Data, London. 47: Hans Verhufen from Focus, Hamburg. 48, 49: Hans W. Silvester from Rapho, Paris. 50: Hans Wiesenhofer, Pöllau, Austria. 53: Thomas Höpker from Agentur Anne Hamann, Munich. 54: H. R. Uthoff from The Image Bank, London. 55: Wilfried Bauer from Agentur Anne Hamann, Munich. 56: Leonard Freed from Magnum. 57: Guido Mangold from Agentur Anne Hamann, Munich. 58: Digitized image by Creative Data, London. 59: Cotton Coulson from Woodfin Camp Inc., Washington, D.C. 60: Jürgen Schadeberg, Le Cannet, France; Cotton Coulson from Woodfin Camp Inc., Washington, D.C. (2). 61: Cotton Coulson from Woodfin Camp Inc., Washington, D.C. 62: Hans Wiesenhofer, Pöllau, Austria — Cotton Coulson from Woodfin Camp Inc., Washington, D.C. 63: Cotton Coulson from Woodfin Camp Inc., Washington, D.C. 64: Hans Wiesenhofer, Pöllau, Austria — Frieder Blickle, Hamburg. 65: Cotton Coulson from Woodfin Camp Inc., Washington, D.C. 66: Jürgen Schadeberg, Le Cannet, France — Fred Grunfeld, Deya, Mallorca. 67: Cotton Coulson from Woodfin Camp Inc., Washington, D.C. — Jürgen Schadeberg, Le Cannet, France. 68: Stephane Duroy from Rapho, Paris. 69: Cotton Coulson from Woodfin Camp Inc., Washington, D.C. 70: Staatsarchiv Hamburg from Bildarchiv Preussischer Kulturbesitz, Berlin. 72: Line drawing from *Germany* by S. Baring-Gould, pub. T. Fisher Unwin, London, 1890. 73: Bildarchiv Preussischer Kulturbesitz, Berlin, from an original manuscript in the Bibliothèque Nationale, Paris. 75-78: Bildarchiv Preussischer Kulturbesitz, Berlin. 79: Illustration by Arthur Rackham, 1900, by kind permission of his daughter Barbara Edwards. 80, 81: Digitized image by Creative Data, London. 82: Alte Pinakothek, Munich, photographed by Lutz Braun from Bildarchiv Preussischer Kulturbesitz, Berlin; Hessische Landesbibliothek, Fulda from Bildarchiv Preussischer Kulturbesitz, Berlin — Bildarchiv Preussischer Kulturbesitz, Berlin. 83: Thomas Höpker from Agentur Anne Hamann, Munich — Daimler-Benz-Museum from Bildarchiv Preussischer Kulturbesitz, Berlin; United Press International — Bildarchiv Preussischer Kulturbesitz, Berlin. 84: Bildarchiv Preussischer Kulturbesitz, Berlin. 85: L. E. Kramer, Member Philatelic Music Circle, U.K. 86-87: Bildarchiv Preussischer Kulturbesitz, Berlin. 88: Bildarchiv Preussischer Kulturbesitz, Berlin (2) — Henry Beville from the Collection of Glenn Sweeting. 89: Heinrich Hoffmann from Bildarchiv Preussischer Kulturbesitz, Berlin — Hugo Jaeger/Life © Time Inc., 1965. 90: The Imperial War Museum, London. 91: Bildarchiv Preussischer Kulturbesitz, Berlin. 92: Frieder Blickle, Hamburg. 94: Roebild, Frankfurt. 95: Hans Verhufen from Focus, Hamburg. 96: Cotton Coulson from Woodfin Camp Inc., Washington, D.C. 97: Frieder Blickle, Hamburg. 98, 99: Thomas Höpker from Agentur Anne Hamann, Munich. 100: Cotton Coulson from Woodfin Camp Inc., Washington, D.C. 101: Horst von Irmer from Internationales Bildarchiv, Munich. 102: Wilfried Bauer from Agentur Anne Hamann, Munich. 103: Timm Rautert, Essen. 104: Friedrich Stark, Dortmund. 106: Timm Rautert, Essen. 107: Digitized image by Creative Data, London. 108: Guido Mangold from Agentur Anne Hamann, Munich. 109: Jamie Simson, Bisley, England. 110: Hans Wiesenhofer, Pöllau, Austria. 112: Frieder Blickle, Hamburg; Thomas Höpker from Agentur Anne Hamann, Munich. 113: Hans Wiesenhofer, Pöllau, Austria. 115: Cotton Coulson from Woodfin Camp Inc., Washington, D.C. 116: Bildarchiv Jürgens, Cologne. 118: Rudi Meisel from VISUM, Hamburg. 119: Horst von Irmer from Internationales Bildarchiv, Munich. 120, 121: David Simson, Bisley, England. 122: Hans Wiesenhofer, Pöllau, Austria; Horst von Irmer from Internationales Bildarchiv, Munich. 123: Sven Simon, Essen. 124: Siegfried Gragnato, Stuttgart. 125: Bildarchiv Jürgens, Cologne. 126: Hans Wiesenhofer, Pöllau, Austria. 128: Rudi Meisel from VISUM, Hamburg. 129: Horst Munzig from Agentur Anne Hamann, Munich. 131: Guido Mangold from Agentur Anne Hamann, Munich. 134-145: Hans Wiesenhofer, Pöllau, Austria. 147: Guido Mangold from Agentur Anne Hamann, Munich. 148: Bildarchiv Jürgens, Cologne. 149: Manfred Vollmer from Focus, Hamburg. 151: Jürgen Schadeberg, Le Cannet, France. 152: Cotton Coulson from Woodfin Camp Inc., Washington, D.C. 155: Guido Mangold from Agentur Anne Hamann, Munich.

BIBLIOGRAPHY

BOOKS

Baedeker's DDR. Stuttgart, 1980.

Bailey, George, and the Editors of Time-Life Books, *Munich.* Time-Life Books, Amsterdam, 1980.

Balfour, Michael:
  The Kaiser and His Times. Pelican Books, London, 1975.
  West Germany. Croom Helm, London, 1982.

Barker, Peter, *Eastern Europe.* Macdonald Educational, London, 1979.

Barraclough, Geoffrey, *The Origins of Modern Germany.* Blackwell, Oxford, 1947.

Berghahn, V. R., *Modern Germany.* Cambridge University Press, Cambridge, 1982.

Botting, Douglas, and the Editors of Time-Life Books, *The Aftermath: Europe.* Time-Life Books, Amsterdam, 1983.

Bryce, James Viscount, *The Holy Roman Empire.* Macmillan, London, 1963.

Bullock, Alan, *Hitler, A Study in Tyranny.* Penguin Books, London, 1971.

Bullough, Donald, *The Age of Charlemagne.* Elek Books, London, 1973.

Central Statistical Board, *Statistical Pocket Book of the German Democratic Republic.* Berlin, 1982.

Childs, David:
  The GDR: Moscow's German Ally. George Allen & Unwin, London, 1983.
  Germany since 1918. Batsford Academic and Educational Ltd., London, 1980.

Chronik der Deutschen. Chronik Verlag, Dortmund, 1983.

Craig, Gordon A., *The Germans.* G. P. Putnam's Sons, New York, 1982.

Cultural Life in the Federal Republic of Germany: A Survey. Inter Nationes, Bonn, 1981.

Cultural Life in the GDR. First-hand information, Panorama DDR, Berlin, 1982.

Dahrendorf, Ralf, *Society and Democracy in Germany.* Weidenfeld and Nicolson Ltd., London, 1968.

Eich, Hermann, *The Unloved Germans.* Trans. by Michael Glenny, Macdonald, London, 1965.

Everyday Life in the GDR. First-hand information, Panorama DDR, Berlin, 1982.

Facts about Germany. Lexikothek Verlag, 1981.

Facts and Figures. A Comparative Survey of the Federal Republic of Germany and the German Democratic Republic, Press and Information Office of the Government of the Federal Republic of Germany, Bonn, 1981.

Families in the GDR. First-hand information, Panorama DDR, Berlin, 1981.

Fodor's Germany. Hodder & Stoughton, London, 1982.

Garland, Henry and Mary, *The Oxford Companion to German Literature.* Clarendon Press, Oxford, 1976.

The German Democratic Republic. Panorama DDR, Berlin, 1982.

Germany. OECD Economic Surveys, 1982-1983, Paris, 1983.

The GDR's Economy in the '80s. First-hand information, Panorama DDR, Berlin, 1981.

Grunfeld, Frederic V., and the Editors of Time-Life Books, *Berlin.* Time-Life Books, Amsterdam, 1977.

Heitzer, Heinz, *GDR: An Historical Outline.* Verlag im Bild, Dresden, 1981.

Holborn, Hajo, *A History of Modern Germany.* Eyre & Spottiswoode, London, 1969.

Jackson, Michael, *The World Guide to Beer.* Mitchell Beazley, London, 1979.

Jones, Alan G., *The Germans: an Englishman's Notebook.* Pond Press, London, 1968.

Klöss, Gunther, *West Germany: An Introduction.* Macmillan Press, London, 1976.

Lau, Alfred, *Bundesrepublik Deutschland.* Univers-Verlag, Bielefeld.

Leonhardt, Rudolf Walter, *This Germany.* New York Graphic Society Publishers Ltd., Greenwich, Connecticut, 1964.

Maehl, William Harvey, *Germany in Western Civilization.* The University of Alabama Press, University, Alabama, 1979.

Mann, Golo, *The History of Germany since 1789.* Chatto and Windus, London, 1968.

Mellor, Roy E. H., *The Two Germanies.* Harper & Row, New York, 1978.

The Military Balance 1982-1983. The International Institute for Strategic Studies, London, 1982.

Morey, George, *West Germany.* Macdonald Educational, London, 1981.

Pasley, Malcolm, ed., *Germany: A Companion to German Studies.* Methuen & Co., London, 1972.

Policies Which Put People First. First-hand information, Panorama DDR, Berlin, 1980.

Prittie, Terence:
  Germany. Life World Library, Time-Life Books, New York, 1962.
  The Velvet Chancellors. Frederick Muller Limited, London, 1979.

Sawers, R., *Life in a West German Town.* Harrap, London, 1974.

Schalk, Adolph, *The Germans.* J. M. Dent & Sons, London, 1972.

Schwarze, Hanns Werner, *The GDR Today.* Oswald Wolff, London, 1973.

Simon, Edith, and the Editors of Time-Life Books, *The Reformation.* Time-Life Books, Amsterdam, 1979.

Speer, Albert, *Inside the Third Reich.* Weidenfeld & Nicholson, London, 1970.

Spindler, George D., *Burgbach: Urbanization and Identity in a German Village.* Holt, Rinehart and Winston, Inc., New York, 1973.

Statistisches Jahrbuch für die Bundesrepublik Deutschland. Statistisches Bundesamt, Wiesbaden, 1982.

Steele, Jonathan, *Socialism with a German Face.* Jonathan Cape, London, 1977.

Tacitus, *The Agricola and the Germania.* Trans. by H. Mattingly and S. A. Handford, Penguin Books, 1982.

Taylor, A.J.P., *The Course of German History.* Methuen, London, 1978.

Tenbrock, Robert-Hermann, *A History of Germany.* Trans. by Paul J. Dine, Longmans, London, 1969.

Wightman, Margaret, *The Faces of Germany.* Harrap, London, 1978.

Wild, Trevor, *West Germany: A Geography of its People.* Longmans, London, 1981.

Youth in the GDR. First-hand information, Panorama DDR, Berlin, 1982.

PERIODICALS

"Are Children a Luxury?" *Scala,* No. 7-8, 1981.

"Dealing with the Angst." *Observer,* December 12, 1982.

"Luther: 500 Years Young." *Time,* October 17, 1983.

"Protest by the New Class." *Time,* February 28, 1983.

"Two Berlins — A Generation Apart." *National Geographic,* January 1982.

"War Without Boundaries." *Time,* October 31, 1977.

INDEX

Page numbers in italics refer to illustrations or illustrated text.

Time-Life Books Inc. offers a wide range of fine recordings, including a *Rock 'n' Roll Era* series. For subscription information, call 1-800-445-TIME, or write TIME-LIFE MUSIC, Time & Life Building, Chicago, Illinois 60611.